Bass Fishing

How to Catch Bass on Plastic Worms

(How to Catch Bass Your First Time on a New Lak)

George Mayer

Published By **Darby Conner**

George Mayer

Bass Fishing: How to Catch Bass on Plastic Worms
(How to Catch Bass Your First Time on a New Lak)

ISBN 978-1-77485-792-2

Legal & Disclaimer

The information contained in this ebook is not designed to replace or take the place of any form of medicine or professional medical advice. The information in this ebook has been provided for educational & entertainment purposes only.

The information contained in this book has been compiled from sources deemed reliable, and it is accurate to the best of the Author's knowledge; however, the Author cannot guarantee its accuracy and validity and cannot be held liable for any errors or omissions. Changes are periodically made to this book. You must consult your doctor or get professional medical advice before using any of the suggested remedies, techniques, or information in this book.

Upon using the information contained in this book, you agree to hold harmless the Author from and against any damages, costs, and expenses, including any legal fees potentially resulting from the application of any of the information provided by this guide. This disclaimer applies to any damages or injury caused by the use and application, whether directly or indirectly, of any advice or information presented, whether for breach of contract, tort, negligence, personal injury, criminal intent, or under any other cause of action.

You agree to accept all risks of using the information presented inside this book. You need to consult a professional medical practitioner in order to ensure you are both able and healthy enough to participate in this program.

Table Of Contents

Chapter 1: What Is a Bass and Why Do You Want to Catch Them?

Fishing for bass is already a popular sport, and it seems that every day it is becoming even more talked about. Are you looking to get into it?If so, then you may not just have questions about how to become great at it, but you might also be curious as to just what the draw is.

The black bass species is a common game fish that has many different offshoots. The most often sought after types are the largemouth bass, the smallmouth bass, and the spotted bass, also known as the Kentucky bass.

So what is the big draw for getting into bass fishing? That's simple: it's a lot of fun! It's like solving a puzzle to find the best places, the best lures, and the best techniques in order to keep catching the quality fish. You will need to think on your feet and switch up your methods anytime the fish seem to be catching on to your style. Entire shows are devoted to this sport, and there are several clubs centered around it as well. Tournaments are set up specifically focusing on the skill of bass fishing. Sometimes there is even cash awarded for winning these.

Most anglers practice catch and release when fishing for bass, however, bass can be quite tasty as well. Generally, the fishermen are simply enjoying the challenge of this sport and enjoying the many aspects of it. You should consider a couple of different things when you have made the decision to become a master of bass fishing, so let's dive right in!

Chapter 2: Where and When to Fish For Bass

When you are starting your journey to becoming a fantastic angler, one of the first things to think about is figuring out just where you should be looking for bass. No matter how fancy your kit or how long you spend on the water, it won't do you any good if you are in completely the wrong type of spot for your prey. So what body of water has the right features for your bass?

Look for an area that has hiding spots for the fish to lurk in. These can include the following:

• Logs

• Rocks

• Trees

• Docks

• Any other structures in the water

A good fishing spot may have a little bit of grass and some rocks or concrete pilings. Since these fish tend to like the more shallow waters, you will likely not want to try casting too deep into the middle of a deep lake. There are some ways that you can also keep track of where others have had some good luck with bass fishing, but make sure you look at how long ago it was.

Join Some Online Groups

Joining some online groups can help point you in the right direction when you are getting started and want to know where to begin. These groups can also share good information on lures, rods, and everything else related to bass fishing.

Check Other Bass Fishing Websites

Different sites on bass fishing will have lists of good lakes for fishing, and many times other anglers will post some as well. The tournaments that go on all over the country also have websites, and you can find some pretty updated information on those too.

Look into Your State Departments

Every state has a Department of Natural Resources, a Department of Wildlife, or something else along those lines. You can usually visit them online or in their physical offices to narrow down your fishing spot.

OK, now that you have decided exactly what body of water is going to be your best bet, you have it all figured out, right? Think again; this is just the beginning. The next step isknowing when exactly to get out on the water to best increase your chances. Not only are there perfect times of the year to be out looking for bass, there are also times of the day that you are more likely to find them.

What Time of Year Is the Best?

Look for your bass during the time of the year right before they start spawning. They will be moving into the shallow areas more often in order to feed even heavier and looking for the right place to nest. Pre-spawn doesn't start in a specific month in every state due to the different climates all over the country. In general, though, it does begin in spring. When the temperature of the water starts to get between 55 and 65 degrees Fahrenheit, this is when you should expect your search to be easier.

What about Time of Day or Weather?

Not only does the season matter, the time of day you are out on the water—in the morning, evening, or right in the middle of the day—matters as well. Bass prefer not to be out in the direct sunlight, so you will have the most luck in the early mornings or the late evenings. If you are trying to search for your prey when it's sunny outside, then you will most certainly want to keep yourself to the spots that have more cover for the fish.

Cloudy days also help bring the bass out more Also, if there is a storm front moving in within the next 24 hours, you might find yourself getting lucky. Mostly, just remember that it's going to be a much more successful fishing trip if you avoid the sun, as the fish will be avoiding it as well.

Chapter 3: The Right Rod and Reel

Now you understand how to narrow down where and when you should be out looking for our fishy friends, but what is the next step? Now you need to make sure that you have the proper gear to become an even greater success. The first thing to take into consideration is your rod. A couple of different types will work great. Different kinds of reels and fishing line and different styles to set them up will ensure your mastery even further.

The Features to Look at When Buying a Rod

Action

The action of a fishing rod describes how flexible or responsive the rod is. It is generally referred to as slow or fast action on either end of the spectrum. When a rod is said to have a faster action, it bends at a point closer to the end of the rod. A slower action means that it will bend at a point closer to the handle. Do not worry if allof this sounds very technical; it really comes down to the fact that a slow-action rod is usually easier for beginners and has a gentler cast. A fast-action rod is much more sensitive, though, which makes it easier to feel when you have a bite. Most bass fishing enthusiasts actually prefer one that has a medium action so that they get the best of both worlds.

Type

The first factor you should focus on in the type of rod is what material it's assembled from. Usually the rods are either manufactured from graphite or fiberglass. Graphite is preferred by most anglers because it is lighter and stiffer.

The most important thing about your rod is that it must fit the kind of reel that you will be using. If you are using a spin cast or bait cast reel, then you will need a casting rod. On the other hand, a spinning rod will be necessary if you are going to use a spinning reel.

Power and Length

The different weights of fishing rods that will work for you will be based on what kind of bass you want to catch. This is also described as the power of a rod. This ranges anywhere from ultra light to extra heavy.

Another factor along the same lines is the length of your rod. The length is generally a consideration for different fishing areas. When it comes to bass fishing, your best choice is most likely going to be a medium rod with the medium action, which we already mentioned. The longer rods are more appropriate for casting long distances, and the shorter heavy rods are best for ocean fishing.

You need to think about the rest of your set up when choosing the proper length because it does all tie together. The weight of line that you are using and the lure size must stay within the limits of your rod length; otherwise it can be damaged or even broken.

So now that you have a bit more knowledge on the right kind of rods needed to achieve your bass fishing goals, let's explore the reels and lines so that you can create the perfect combination and come out on top.

What Is the Right Kind of Reel?

There are three main styles to look at when choosing the proper reel for your angling needs.

Your skill level will play a large role when making your choice.

Spin cast Reel

A spin cast reel is very simple, and even a fishing beginner can use one with ease. However, they are not always the most appropriate choice for bass fishing.

Spinning Reel

A spinning reel goes on the underside of a spinning rod. This design makes it easier to use a lightweight line and to cast further distances than will the other styles.

Bait cast Reel

This is, by far, your best choice in reels for bass fishing. This type of reel enables you to cast with more accuracy and is better for the heavier lures that you will need. This reel is also specifically designed for angling in vegetation and for large fish.

Chapter 4: Choosing the Right Lure

The next thing for you to decide on is what lure will suit you and your goals the best. First, remember that bass are extremely curious and are attracted to noise. That being said, there are five main types of lures that are the most recommended for successful bass fishing.

Crank baits

These noisy lures will be best for fishing within areas that have rocky bottoms and a little bit of vegetation. Look for short, fat styles, and get some that are deep diving, shallow diving, and medium diving. Try having a selection on hand that are bright, but make sure they are the right colors for what your fish are eating in your area. Also, try some with eyes so that the bass can locate them better.

Spinner baits

Spinner baits also have a nice, attractive rattle to them and are designed to work well in the same areas with a small amount of vegetation and some rockiness on the bottom. Look for some of these with flashy gold blades, and get some in black, white, and chartreuse with other blades to mix it up. Spinners have a weed less option you can purchase that makes them especially nice for areas that have a lot of vegetation. However, they are more difficult to get your hook into.

Plastics or Jigs

These are plastic worms and bait that you would use to get the bass to bite. You want to get dark colors in varying sizes and some hooks and sinkers as well. When using this type of bait, the movement that attracts your prey comes from you and your rod as opposed to the lure itself. Once you drop the lure, you will raise it up for a moment and then let it drop again. Plastic bait is extremely versatile, and you can easily use this type to fish in areas that have a lot of vegetation growing in.

Top water Lures

This type of lure is your best bet when angling in shallow areas. They are also appropriate in areas that have features like lily pads. You will need to get different sizes and colors for your top water lures. The colors will correspond with the different seasons to attract the fish throughout the year. You need bright colors in the spring months and muted colors in the fall and winter seasons. You can also find lures with patterns that are made to simulate frogs or lizards. Just make sure to pay attention to what the bass are feeding on in the location that you are fishing in.

Live Bait

Not only are there a variety of artificial lures, as mentioned above, but bass also enjoy biting when you angle with live bait. You can use worms, of course. They like them to be a little salty. Some other options include frogs, minnows, and night crawlers.

Chapter 5: Finishing Touches to Ensure Your Success

Have you realized yet that the sport of bass fishing is actually more complicated than many people might think? It requires skill, planning, and the ability to think on your feet. Having the right gear set-up for your time on the water helps immensely, and knowing where and when to look can make or break your day. Let's go over some more little tips to keep you catching those big ones!

Pay Attention to What the Fish are Biting

If you are having a lot of luck with one type of lure, then by all means keep using it. But the bass may decide that they are tired of that one, so do remain flexible to change. Have a variety of your favorite lures and bait with you and switch it up when they become accustomed to one or when they just get tired of it.

Look at Their Feeding Habits

You will want to find out what the bass are eating in their habitat. Doing so can be a great help. When you catch one, look into its mouth as it is struggling. Occasionally, the fish will throw up and this can help you determine what your best bet for lures should be based on what they are feeding on.

Don't Become a Statue!

Say you have tried switching up your lures and you know that there are bass just waiting to be caught in your lake or pond, but you can't get any. What do you do now? Move! Don't just stay in a place where they don't feel like biting; that won't get you anywhere.

Try Some Different Techniques

There is wide variety of techniques that you can try to get the bass to bite at a line that they are not into going after. These include drop shotting, wacky fishing, jig fishing, float fishing, split shotting, and dragging. Every time you are in a different location or in a different climate for different bass, you have to be able to find what best suits them in particular. Don't be afraid to try something new or different; being open to innovation will lead to you having more luck in your angling.

The Size of Your Lure Doesn't Lead to the Size of Your Catch

Just because you have a large lure, it doesn't mean that you will catch a larger bass. If you aren't getting anything with your lure, try a smaller one and see if that makes a difference. Sometimes just the small changes make a huge difference in whether or not you are getting just a tan or catching actual bass.

Look at the Maps

Each body of water has a map letting you know where outcroppings, drop-offs, and other landmarks are. Utilizing a map beforehand can be essential in letting you know what part of the lake you need to be on. Remember what kind of areas the bass like to lurk in, and then you can zero in on them.

Wrapping It All Up

The first step to becoming great at the sport of bass fishing is to make sure that you know where you will be looking for your prey. Do some research on this, and connect with some other anglers to narrow this down a little. If catfish are the only thing living in the lake that you are exploring, then obviously you aren't going to catch a whole lot of bass in that body of water. It's just pure logic there.

You should also consider joining online forums or bass fishing clubs to connect with other anglers. You can gather and share a lot of information that way, and they can really be a lot of fun as you get more into your new sport. Not only are forums and clubs a source of information, but you can make some new friends to share in your interest and help you find more fish! But remember, not only are there clubs and websites, there are also countless television shows and some radio shows, and you can even start joining tournaments so you can compete with other bass fishers.

Your next concern should be your gear. Look for a rod that is medium length with a medium action. This helps ensure that you can really pull in those big bass with no problems. Not having the right rod will just be setting yourself up for frustration. If the rod is too short, you won't be able to cast into the areas you want to. If it is too long, then it will simply become an irritation and you run the risk of breaking it with the lures and line weight that you will need to use. The right rod means that you can attach the right reel and use the right lure for bass.

One thing that some bass anglers use is a fish-finding device. We didn't really cover technology, but you can certainly invest in one if you think it will be helpful. This is definitely not a necessity for you to become a bass fishing pro, but it is another available option.

After you have the proper rod and reel, you need to gather a good collection of lures that are made specifically tailored for catching bass. You will want a varied collection on hand for those different situations and the different locations that you will be visiting. Don't be afraid of change! One of the most important things that you can remember is that you will often have to change your methods to continue catching the fish that you are after.

Give some of the varied techniques a try. Don't just get set in the same habits of throwing the same lure over and over again into the same spot and waiting. Doing that won't get you anywhere as far as reeling in the bass. When someone mentions something new that he or she has tried, give it a shot to see if it works for you as well.

Finally, remember to have fun! Fun is the whole reason that you are getting into bass fishing in the first place. Enjoy the ride, don't be afraid to change things, and make sure that you have the right tools for the job. Gathering information and getting your gear together can be just as fun as actually fishing. Angling for bass is more like a big puzzle that you get to put together. You should really enjoy every part of this process.

You can easily achieve everything in this book. You should certainly be well on your way by this point to becoming the next bass fishing master. This can be an awesome new journey for you, and hopefully you will love every minute of it!

All about the Bass

Bass. Imagine how it looks like. Aside from the stringed instrument, you are most likely to picture a fish with a large mouth and dark green silvery scales, which is most likely the largemouth bass or Micropterus salmoides. However, you can find many other bass species both in freshwater and saltwater. Bass fishes include the black fin seabass (Lateolabrax latus), Choctaw bass (M. haika), European bass (Dicentrarchus labrax), Guadalupe bass (M. treculii), Japanese seabass (Lateolabrax japonicas), largemouth bass (Micropterus salmoides), smallmouth bass (M. dolomieu), striped bass (Morone saxatilis), spotted bass (M. punctulatus), and white bass (M. chryops). The most popular among fishermen and anglers though is the largemouth bass.

Along with tuna, swordfish, marlin, and tarpon, largemouth bass belongs to the most popular game fishes in North America. They have a rather distinct appearance with their olive green scales and dark, yellowish, jagged strips that run horizontally along their flanks. This impressive game fish has a lifespan of 16 years in the wild, and the current maximum-recorded length reached nearly 30 inches with a weight of 22 pounds. The typical diet of a largemouth bass is somewhat diverse. They could eat crawfish, baitfish, shrimp, scuds, frogs, and insects. Their remarkably strong and elongated jaws are capable of catching and eating large preys that are half of their size.

Bass fishing has evolved into a billion-dollar industry in North America.This evolution of modern bass fishing in the United States was not subjected to the booming angling development flourishing in Europe, South Africa, and Asia. In fact, anglers in Europe learned techniques for lure fishing from US fishermen. Black bass is, arguably, the second most preferred game fish following blue marlin, and it has greatly influenced the development of fishing gears including lures, lines, reels, rods, fish finding instruments, electronic depth gage, specialized fishing boats, float tubes, and drift boats.

Its humble beginnings started with the working-class fly anglers using poles and live baits. Today, it has become a national sport for anglers. It was in the middle of the 19th century when bass fishing used its first artificial lure in the form of an artificial fly.Subsequently, heavier flies were developed specifically for bass fishing. Spinners, wooden lures or plugs made of lightweight cork, and plastic worms were introduced to fishermen. The production of these plastic worms transformed bass fishing as a sport in the United States.

When the railroad system developed and expanded, largemouth bass and smallmouth bass fishes were suddenly stocked outside their local ranges. The sport advanced so dramatically that shippers and steam engines had to device ingenious ways to transport the species in various towns and water stops. New towns were purposely established for bass fishing. The government, the Department of Agriculture in particular, started assisting farmers in their construction of ponds and even started offering guidance in the management of these fishponds. Environmentalists and conservation groups teamed up with fishermen and the government to introduce and promote black bass as a fishing sport. Its popularity thrived in the fact that largemouth bass is one of the few species who could survive in waters that are too murky and too warm for other game fishes.

There was a great man who was seriously inspired with the idea of making bass fishing into a sport. In the 1960s, Ray Scott, also called the godfather of modern bass fishing, had this brilliant idea while watching a basketball game in his motel room in Jackson, Mississippi. He began drafting the rules for the competition. Scott was careful to include the safety, conservation, and principles of ethical angling which are still the same fundamentals used today. In 1968, Ray Scott officially established the Bass Anglers Sportsman Society (B.A.S.S.). Don Butler from Oklahoma became its first member and he paid $100 for a lifetime membership. B.A.S.S' first Bassmaster Magazine was published a year later. From then on to the present year, bass pro fishing tournament has become one of the highly anticipated events every year. The longest standing record in bass fishing is held by George Perry in 1932 when he caught a 22 pound 4 ounce bass in Montgomery

Lake, Georgia and this record tied exactly with Manabu Kurita from Lake Biwa, Aichi, Japan in 2009.

A question hangs in the air though. Why would you go bass fishing? The answer is: Why not? There are thousands of reasons to go bass fishing. Currently, bass fishing is one of the best freshwater sport in the United States and this industry will only grow bigger as the years pass. As this industry gets larger, so does the opportunities. Anglers are not the only ones benefitting from this business. Careers are now offered in the retail industry. Tournament lecturers, advertisers, and charters have found opportunities for success in bass fishing.

The personal aspect of bass fishing could probably outweigh its business side. This outdoor sport will help you discipline yourself on an equally competitive level as anyone involved in professional sports like basketball or football. The patience needed to master the professional techniques and skills is no joke. Brains are as essential as brawns in bass fishing. The mental puzzles an angler has to solve just to understand the fish can be a little tedious, but very rewarding. Don't forget the spirit of sportsmanship that it can bring. Those who are in competitive angling build a solid friendship and comradeship with fellow anglers. Relationships, including family and friends, improved through fishing. The excitement, the laughter, and the enjoyment of bass fishing have brought loved ones closer. Then think of the outdoors, you get to enjoy the wildlife and the beauty that nature has to offer.

Now let's get to the particulars. What does bass fishing offer? Bass anglers are addicted to the sport because they can always be on the go whether they carry big or small gears. Even without a large bass boat, you can go fishing along the bank or in your small rubber boat. There is no real need to purchase fancy bait and lures. Bass love earthworms, so just dig around the mud and you'll surely get your pail full. Finding a bass lake is not as difficult as you may think; in fact, you can find them just about anywhere there's water. Just gather your friends and family and pitch your gear.

The tournaments are festive events. The 75 mph boat ride is something you can hardly forget. Fishing beside the best anglers in the world may get your competitive streak on full mode. The explosive strike of a voracious bass is a sight to see. It's a great pound for pound experience. Even if you don't catch anything, the excitement is still there because you really never know when you'll catch one. Don't forget the unforgettable weigh-ins.

You can really do this even when you're old or if you want to bring your children along. That's the beauty of bass fishing. It is an extraordinary experience for anyone of any age. There's more to bass fishing than meets the eye. Read on and discover the satisfaction of this favorite sport.

Tackle and Gear

To succeed in most things, you must start with the basics. In bass fishing, it doesn't mean spending thousands of dollars on a boat, unless you can afford it. All you really need are your essential equipment and your correct approach. In this chapter, you'll find the basic bass fishing tackle and gear list. These tools are decent enough to help you get started on bass fishing and to help you for any possibility on a fishing trip.

Rod. - Other than your fishing license, the first obvious thing you'll need is an excellent rod. You can find several different types of rods in your local tackle shops, and they vary in price, size, and weight. If you want to start with bank fishing, a medium-action spinning rod with medium length is the perfect choice. You need to get a spinning rod for easy casting, especially on days when the weather is not too accommodating. Yes, it sounds more like what an experienced angler would use, but this problem solver rod will help you throw lighter lures for longer distances. Longer casts mean better catches as a starter. If you're looking to fish in tight corners, you may want to choose a short spinning rod. This type of rod will help you avoid cat tails and other bank interferences.

Line - For a beginner in bass fishing, it's not advisable to buy relatively costly lines. You will be making a few mistakes every now and then.

It would be best to shed off a few dollars on economical lines rather than splurging on expensive lines. Your first snag could cut you off as long as 30 yards and a line is one gear that you always change out after every few trips. For smaller lures, try using low-cost standard lines before buying braids or copolymers. Standard lines are good learning tools when you're starting to fish for bass.

Tackle Box - You clearly need an assortment of lures, especially on a great fishing day. Whether you're on a boat or on the bank, mobility is a must. You need a stocked tackle box that's easy to haul. Carrying a heavy tackle box is not a good idea, especially for beginners. You can always start with the smaller "pocket" tackle boxes that aren't longer than 8 inches. Find tackle boxes with compartments on both sides. They should be capable of storing enough lures for at least half a day's worth of fishing. It's easier to carry around on your belt and you could run fast even with a full line.

Hooks, Terminal Tackles, and Weights - Hooks are absolute must-haves in your tackle box. The right hook will help you catch more bass on your fishing trips. You will most likely find several different hooks in your local tackle shops, but first look for worm hooks. Worm hooks are classic and essential. They are a little bit pricy than other hooks, but the great thing about them is that they wouldn't need sharpening. The little point is razor sharp and, for that alone, it is worth the price. Don't forget to purchase a hook remover for some stubborn fishes who like to eat up hooks. Remember to pick up some terminal tackles and weights on your way. Terminal tackles like split rings and swivels, are vital for creating rigs and eliminating line twists. You'd also need two types of weights: drop shot weights and bullet head weights. These different weights are considered necessary for fishing in different depths. The preferred basic weight for bass fishing is ¼ of an ounce because it is applicable in almost every fishing depth.

Fishing Boats - You don't need to purchase a $30,000 bass boat right away. Arm yourself with an appropriate boat for your fishing needs. If you're going to fish on small town lakes, go easy on the motor. Equip yourself instead with quality rods, reels, and fishing line. However, going big time on bass boats comes with its advantages. You can definitely bring most of your equipment with you, like electronic thermometers, depth-finders, live wells, trolling motors, etc.

These fishing tackle and gears are the basic stuff you'll need to get you up and running for bass fishing. On the other hand, here are a few additional items you might not want to forget for your own comfort:

•Consider putting on some sunblock and polarized sunglasses for those long and hot trips.

• You can use either a lip gripper or landing net when catching bass. It all depends on the size of the fish.

• Needle nose pliers are used for unhooking the fish.

• Get a knife or a multi-tool for your go-to device.

• Don't underestimate the use of fish handling gloves. It's always best to avoid punctures and cuts from hooks and fish teeth.

• Bass fishing is fun but it can get tough. Be prepared with your first aid kit to treat common fishing injuries.

• Clean your hands, gear, and tackle with towels and rags.

• Lures are relatively expensive and the fish can snag anytime. Make sure to use a lure retriever to ensnare the lure's hook and save you from buying a new set.

• You might need a clipper for cutting a tippet after tying your knot or changing a hook.

• There is a possibility of getting your lines broken or tangled so make sure to bring along extra, heavier, and more durable fishing lines. Take some pre-made leaders as well. It's the material between your bait and your fishing line. Quality pre-made leaders could mean the difference between a successful fishing trip and a disappointment.

• Remember to haul in your rod holders, stringers, and bait bucket for the live baits. There is comfort and efficiency in organization even when bass fishing.

• Get a cast net if you are plan on catching live baits.

• Bass fishing in the dark sounds daring and exciting but it could get tedious and exhausting. Bring your flashlight and catch that bass.

•Bring your fish scale, measuring device, and camera along to record your achievements.

These basic gears are efficient, easy on the hands, and can simply get the job done. Begin with these basic bass fishing equipment. When your skills improve, slowly upgrade your equipment.

Lure Them In

The amount of bass lures on the market is enough to make a beginner's head spin. They come in so many styles, sizes, and colors that can overwhelm even the most experienced of anglers. You are just starting to fill your tackle box and all you need are a few simple lures for a solid lure arsenal. Different lures are needed for varied situations, including the mood of the fish and the body of water. The majority of lures present in this chapter are for starters but even if after you become an expert angler, they will still be present in your tackle box.

Crankbaits - It doesn't matter where you choose to fish, be it from the boat or on the bank, using a crankbait will always result in a catch. Nonetheless, crankbaits are more than a cast-and-retrieve lure. You have to vary your retrieve to catch a bass effectively. Move the crankbait erratically by twitching it, reeling it, and knocking it especially when you are targeting an aggressive bass. You can't simply cast and reel it straight. This will leave you empty handed. Experts recommend using natural-colored crankbaits when fishing on clear water and flashy colors in murky waters.

Spinnerbait - Spinnerbaits are great for beginners because of its simple cast-and-straight-reel quality. It gives you an advantage if you want to cover a lot of water in a limited time. The cast-and-reel feature won't allow you to be idle because if you stop reeling, the spinnerbait will just stop performing. The vibration and flash you create when reeling in attracts bass, which makes it perfect for beginners. All you need to do is raise and lower the rod when retrieving from deep waters. Get a few smaller spinnerbaits when you are just starting to get more strikes. It may get you smaller bass but it will get you more fish. A catch is still a catch. In the future, gradually upgrade to larger spinnerbaits for bigger bass catch.

Topwater - Topwater is a bass fishing surface lure. This type of lure could be the most exciting way to catch a bass. There is simply nothing like watching a big, mean bass break the water surface to catch the lure. Topwater lure floats and uses water disruption and noise along the water surface to attract the bass below. To effectively catch a bass, be quick on your toes for a fast retrieve and raise your rod tip.

Popper lures - Popper lures are the cast and sit type. Sometimes the "pop" triggers happen every few seconds. Other times, there is constant chugging in the end. However, there will be periods of long waits before you can see any chugging action. The popping noise, the jerk on the rod tip, and surface disruption still depend on the bass activity in the area. Start with poppers that are just a quarter ounce in weight and two to three inches long. They are small but you can cast them farther.

Soft-plastics - The best way to begin bass fishing is by using rubber worms or plastic worms. Anybody can cast plastic and rubber worms. They can deceive a fish with a great possibility of catching a big bass. It's probably safe to say that soft plastics have perfectly mimicked forage. Plastic worms have caught more fish than any other bait there is. Look for soft jerk baits. They may be difficult to rig at first, but it wouldn't take long for you to master it. If you feel like your casting skill is not that accurate yet, this is the bait for you. You can cast plastic worms anytime and anywhere. It's all about keeping your line tight and feeling the soft vibration from the worm when it lands on and in the water.

Torpedo lures - Torpedo lures are also known as propeller lures or prop baits. Torpedo lures have propellers driven by water resistance. These propellers are powered while being pulled through the water. They make a rippling sound when it touches the water surface and this sound attracts the attention of the bass. The first method you can try when using torpedo lures is to simply cast and straight retrieve.

Live bait - In bass fishing, live bait is the classic, but still efficient way to catch a fish. Largemouth bass, in particular, are more likely attracted and more likely to strike live bait rather than an artificial bait, especially after a storm or a cold front. You can use frogs, leeches, minnows, and crayfish for starters. For a beginner who wants to fish on the bank, just use live baits, and use other fish attractants later. When you are ready for deep fishing and you have the proper rig, try other varieties of lures and baits.

Tips, Tricks, and Tactics

Bass is a popular game fish because it is more abundant than other species. Nonetheless, just because it's available doesn't mean you can easily haul a number on your boat. Bass fishing is more than just tossing bait and waiting for a fish to bite. Whether you want to be a tournament angler or a leisure angler, you still need some critical techniques to optimize your fishing performance.

One of the unspoken rules of fishing is: Do not disturb the waters. When the bass in the area are hiding, do not spook the fish. Go into stealth mode. The best techniques you can use in this situation are pitching and flipping. Start with the easier technique which is pitching. Ensure that you let out enough line to keep even with the reel. Press the button and keep your reel open. Don't let go of the thumb pressing the reel spoon. Carefully lower your rod tip on the water and use your free hand to grab the lure. Swing your rod tip upwards, remove the thumb from your reel spool, and in one swift motion, let go of your lure. Practice the timing of these steps until you could accurately slingshot your bait. Quickly close your reel once it lands on the water because bass are known to strike rapidly.

Flipping is more precise than pitching, but it takes a lot of practice before you can master it. Let out a longer line of about 15 feet before you close the reel. Extend your arm and start pulling the line between first rod guide and the reel. When you raise your rod, the bait could swing towards your direction so be careful. Swing the bait towards your target like a pendulum. Don't stop feeding the line in your hand while swinging. Remember to tighten the slack and wait for the strike. The angle may seem awkward but it's perfect in catching a hiding bass.

When using soft plastic, the ideal technique partner is dragging. Dragging is easy, but as a technique, it may require the use of a Carolina rig. This rig consists of a sinker, beads, main line, leader, brass clacker, swivel, and a plastic lure. Choose your target area and pitch your bait upwind. Let the bait sink to the bottom and hold your line tightly while your boat drifts. This technique can be used for any season of the year but best utilized during spring time. It's best to use dragging in deep waters and when you have a wide area to work in.

Drop shooting is a finesse form of fishing technique. It was clearly designed for catching the fussiest bass when fishing in clear water. It is a simple and efficient method using light tackle and soft lure. Reel up your worm and let the sinker bounce along the bottom. Let the worm dangle a few inches above the water surface and leave it free for the bass to take. The length between your sinker and the worm depends on the murkiness of the water bottom. You may also want to consider your choice of height suspension. It could just be a few inches to a full foot. Make your bait dance on the side of your boat and don't worry about the retrieve right away. There's always a hungry bass willing to take a bite.

Learning the diverse techniques makes you a better angler. It can infinitely increase your enjoyment in your bass fishing trips. On the other hand, it wouldn't hurt to succeed in the business as well, so here are a few tips and tricks than could promote you from beginner to pro.

Use the pre-spawn period for fishing bass. If you want to score the gold pot, fish when the water temperature reaches 65 degrees in spring. Bass will move to shallow areas closer to shore. Always remember to release female bass so they could continue the cycle.

Study your water map. Correctly identify the drop-offs, depths, and sunken areas where the bass might be utilizing as shelter. Bring your map every time you are out on the water and mark the areas where you deemed a fishing success or a failure.

Save all your torn plastic worms. They may be shredded, but you can still use them for shallow water fishing. Bass love to attack prey they consider injured. Likewise, use baits with a pinkish or reddish head. They can fool the fish into thinking that your bait is wounded.

Sharpen your hooks - Boney jaws require sharper hooks so make sure all your hooks are sharpened before going on a trip. Your hooks should be capable of penetrating the bass' jaws.

Keep an eye on your line - Check your lines for frays. It's common for line to get a little tattered when bumping into rocks, stumps, or branches. Examine your lines to avoid breaking and losing your prized catch.

Familiarize yourself with the habits of bass - When the weather is clear and the sun is bright, bass will look for a cover. Try to locate possible areas where the bass could be using as a shelter. When there is an overcast sky, bass will come out of their shelter. If it's windy, face the wind. Bass will always swim in the direction of the water's current so make it easier for them to find your bait. When a storm is about to set in, fish before the front comes. The pressure of the anticipated storm excites the bass and it makes them active. Remember not to move during the storm for your own safety.

 "Poke" and bug the bass - They can get cranky and you have to convince them several times to bite into your hook. Try tossing your lures several times even on the same location until you get a bite.

Timing is everything - The ideal time to fishing is always in the early hours of the morning and the early evening. Bass will feed during these hours so it's best to take your fishing gear at that time. You might as well enjoy the sunrise and the sunset.Fishing could be a laid-back job but it could get pretty active when you're on a hunt for some large, aggressive bass. It could test your patience and your skill. This is where your bass fishing techniques comes in handy. These few tricks of the trade are critical to your success and performance as an angler or even as a weekend bass fisherman.

Location, Location, Location

Now that you are fully equipped, where do you go from here? For a beginner, going deep is not necessarily the ideal way. It's always best to start in shallow waters. Smaller ponds may offer smaller bass, but it is the perfect hunting ground if you want to practice. Some ponds or lakes may be private so get permission first from the landowner before fishing. Getting arrested is not how you want to start your fishing trip. The property is not yours so thread carefully and respectfully.

If you want to look for nearby ponds and lakes, the web is your best bet for identifying the bodies of water. Try your Google maps or use Fishidy, a great fishing social network where you can find information on some of the best fishing maps. Fellow anglers will even share with you the hot spots in the area and might even give you some tips on how to catch the "big ones".

However, if you don't want to rely on technology, and you want to hone your hunting instincts by yourself instead, ask yourself this: "If I were a bass, where would I hide?" Where do you find this ornery fish? Bass loves to hide and seek shelter. The best way to catch them is to find where they nest. In shallow waters, bass are most likely to hide under structures like boat docks or below plants like water lilies. When the rocky bottom of the pond or the lake becomes sandy, try casting somewhere near the hydrilla or waterweeds. These are some of the favorite hiding places of bass. If this still fails, just cast almost anywhere and give luck a chance. Trying is the first step to success.

Bass fishing can be as easy as casting right on the bank. Take a calm stroll along the banks of creeks and rivers. When you're on the bank, silence is the golden rule. Obviously, you can talk but don't make a racket. Walk quietly and do not stomp on the ground or you'll spook the bass away. A bass is extremely sensitive to prey, lures, and predators. He'll be making a quick escape as soon as he hears your noise. On that note, don't wear crimson-colored clothes, similar hues, or any unnatural color. Bass may identify you as a predator. Wear your earth tones like brown, green, or dark blue to be inconspicuous.

Boat docks and boat ramps are like safe havens for bass. The shade and the access to almost unlimited food in these areas make up for all the commotion of the place. Marinas and dock owners may allow you to fish right on the dock but try casting on piling rows or corners. Quietly observe where the bass may take residence and you're sure to get an ample catch right where you're standing.

One of the unusual but best places to catch a bass is on a riprap or rock armor. Ripraps are the chunks of concrete or stones you'll see on an embankment slope of bridges or roadways. They were designed to prevent erosion. If you look closely, there are crevices and holes with water underneath. These holes usually continue even under water. The ideal fishing spot is on the side where the current is sweeping. Cast your lure in the same direction of the current. The ripraps of power dams could be one of the best places for catching bass. The swift current will carry the scent of your bait right towards the bass. You'll see how quick the bass latches on to the smell.

There a few smaller but nonetheless remarkable places to catch bass like strip pits or smaller ponds which receive less water pressure. They could be too small for a boat but ample enough for the largemouth bass to settle in. Don't overlook these places. This could be where your gold pot is. There is ample opportunity in every water body you may encounter. Luck could play a part but it all boils down to your patience and persistence. If you are itching to explore the big bad water world, here are a few suggestions for your next bass fishing trip.

Grand Lake O' the Cherokees, Oklahoma - The life cycle of bass thrives in this area and this water could be the perfect lake for beginners. New anglers are grateful for the bass generosity of this lake.

Dale Hollow Lake, Kentucky/Tennessee - Home to some of the world's best record in International Game Fish Association, this lake hosts a number of sizable and extremely strong largemouth bass. Smallmouth bass and several game fishes are available here for all four seasons.

Kissimmee Chain of Lakes, Florida - This is a favorite among many anglers because of the bass fishing tournaments held here. The largemouth bass that resides here lives quite well to its name "Large". Its size alone is enough to make you pack that gear this instant.

Lake Coeur d'Alene, Idaho - This magnificent lake allows you to fish for bass in several ways. You can go as deep as 40 feet in boulders and ledges or you can easily go for a fish on the banks.

Lake Champlain, Vermont - Monster largemouth bass and feisty smallmouth bass are both plentiful in Lake Champlain. This enormous lake has several fishing spots and the best quality bass have been known to reside here.

Lake St. Clair, Michigan - Visit this top bass lake during summer season and you'll be "gladly" welcomed by a number of big fishes, including the largemouth bass.

Lake Erie, Ohio/New York - Largemouth bass may be tricky to catch here but the amount of smallmouth bass in this lake is enough for any angler. Pre-spawn season could be your lucky time for catching the elusive largemouth bass.

Sam Rayburn Reservoir, Texas - This southeast Texas reservoir has recovered greatly from years of drought. The water has risen steadily and it has brought in a great amount of bass.

Smith Mountain Lake, Virginia - Both largemouth bass and smallmouth bass are abundant in the area. You'll get a good share of quality catch at the end of the day.

Thousand Islands, New York - You can come here for its sheer beauty but it's also a famous hatchery for smallmouth bass. These smallmouth bass will quench your thirst for adventure because they are fairly "spirited" bass and will fight hard for your bait. A bass fishing trip is a great thrilling experience for anyone. Visit these places and indulge your bass fisherman persona. There's always a perfect place for your personality and your preferred catch. If excitement and satisfaction is all you want, pack those fishing arsenal right now!

Chapter 6: Bass fishing essentials

Bass fishing is an angling activity performed for recreational and competitive purposes. The species belonging to the black bass category are among the most popular choices for gamefish, with the largemouth bass standing at the top of the preference list. Even though the black bass is considered a native species in North America, more recently, it has been introduced into other countries, as it enjoys an increased popularity as gamefish.

The largemouth bass is a freshwater gamefish, being also known as Micropterus Salmoides and it belongs to the Sunfish family. These species of black bass are known after different names, including the widemouth bass, green trout and Florida bass. Given its extensive popularity as a gamefish, the black bass has been chosen as the state fish of different states in America, including Georgia, Florida and Alabama.

It is easy to recognize the largemouth bass due to its olive-green or gray color, marked by the horizontal black stripe, found on each flank. The stripe is actually composed from black blotches and it may vary from one fish to the other. The largemouth bass can also be recognized after its prominent jaw; also, one can make the difference between females and males, by taking into account the size of the fish. It is known that the females are larger in size than the males, especially the ones that are breeding.

From the different types of black bass fish that exist, the largemouth is considered to be one of the largest. It can grow as far as 75 cm in length and reach an impressive weight of 11.4 kg (even though the biggest recorded largemouth bass is known to have had 10.12 kg, being caught by a Japanese angler in 2009, at the Lake Biwa, in Japan). A similar record was made in 1932, when an angler caught a largemouth bass of 10.09 kg, in Lake Montgomery (Georgia). On average, the largemouth bass can live around 16 years.

Today, it is encouraged that angles apply the practice of catch and release, so as to protect the existing population of largemouth bass. This is even more important when an angler catches a large specimen; this is because the larger specimens are actually females and these are breeding. By catching these specimens and not releasing them back into the water, one may have a negative impact on the population of the largemouth bass in the future.

The good news is that the largemouth bass responds well to the practice of catch and release but you will have to handle it with extreme care. In fact, the largemouth bass is one of the most popular species of fish and expert anglers often use a wide range of gear in order to enjoy their hobby. The truth is that the industry has advanced very much in the past few years and, today, beginners into the world of bass fishing have all sort of fishing gear available. In another chapter, you will find information related to the most essential fishing gear that you can use for bass fishing, including: rods, reels, lines and lures. You might also discover that you can use newer technologies, including those for measuring the depth of the water and to locate the fish. You will surely need a boat and other accessories, so be sure to read that chapter with attention.

There is one very good reason why the black bass, and the largemouth bass, is such a popular gamefish. This is related to the fact that the largemouth bass will fight to be released, once it is caught. Anglers simply love the excitement that the largemouth bass provides when fighting, especially when see the fish in the air, making a large effort in order to escape from the hook. In general, the largemouth bass prefers to hide in shallow waters, especially where there are a lot of weeds. As you start your adventure into the world of bass fishing, you will see that this fish prefers a run that is both short and powerful; it will try to hide, not only where there are weed beds or patches but also behind submerged logs.

The popularity of the black bass has led to the introduction of these species all over the world. Today, there are many angling sporting competitions dedicated to the catch and release of the largemouth bass. In general, one may keep the smaller fish but the larger ones always have to be released, due to the reasons specified above. The meat of the largemouth bass is white and mushy in consistency, with a mild taste when cooked.

In case you are wondering about the sources of freshwater where you can find the largemouth bass, you should know that this fish is commonly found in lakes, reservoirs and ponds. You can also find it in rivers, creeks or streams. The largemouth bass will always be found in waters of high quality and also where there is a generous quantity of food. Knowing what kind of food the largemouth bass prefers, you will also be able to choose better baits.

Even though the largemouth bass can provide a lot of entertainment when caught, you should keep in mind that this is not an easy fish to catch. It is a predator fish, equipped with a strong sense of smell and high visual acuity. You can easily lose this fish by bringing strong smells at the site, such as tobacco. Placing your hand in the water, after touching certain things (cigarettes included), will also alert the largemouth bass that you are in the area.

In regard to the angling competitions, you should know that the largemouth bass fish that are caught are first weighed and then released. You will have to take good care of the fish until the time of measurement, as anglers are disqualified and penalized if the fish dies. Sometimes, treatment can be applied for the different injuries, before the fish is released into the water.

Chapter 7: Bass fishing gear

Nowadays, there are a lot of great choices when it comes to fishing gear. However, you must know which of the many types of equipment available are recommended for bass fishing. This chapter is dedicated to the physical equipment you should consider using for largemouth bass fishing. Read it until the end and organize your shopping list.

The fish hook is one of the most essential items to add to the list, being used for the impaling of the fish in the mouth. In some cases, the hook can be used to snag the fish out of the water, from the body. You will see that the fish hook has to be attached to the fishing line, different types of lures being used to attract the attention of the fish. Just a simple look at an online store will reveal the greatest variety of fishing hooks but you have to remember that not all of them are suitable for bass fishing.

In general, you can consider the hooks that can hold a largerbait, including artificial lures (such as worms) and even the ones that rotate, so that they penetrate the mouth of the bass through the roof. Don't be quick in choosing the biggest hook you come across and always consider the type of bait you will be using for the bait. Also, don't be quick to pay the additional fee to sharpen your hook; you can purchase a cheap file and handle such matters yourself.

The fishing line is just as important as the hook, being made from different types of materials, such as nylon, dacron or polyethylene. It is recommended that you chose a fishing line that is made from single-strand monofilament, as this will hold better under pressure. In deciding on the best fishing line for your needs, you will need to take certain features into consideration, such as: length, material and weight. Keep in mind that, if you choose a line that is more resistant and thicker, this also means it will be more visible in the water.

A good fishing line should provide an increased strength to breaking, resisting to the constant exposure to the sun and stretch under pressure. You should also consider the resistance to abrasion and the visibility potential when deciding on a fishing line.

Anglers also use fishing lines that are made from fluorocarbon– given the fact that these have a higher density, they are less visible under water. However, the fishing lines that are made from fluorocarbon are also more rigid, which means that they are not so easy to maneuver as those that are made from monofilament. The advantages of the fluorocarbon fishing lines include the increased resistance to abrasion and the reduced water absorbance rate (in comparison to the ones made from monofilament). Another choice is represented by the braided fishing lines, these being recommended for the fishing of largemouth bass in areas where there is a lot of vegetation or submerged logs.

Apart from the fishing hook and line, you will also need sinkers, these being small or larger weights that are used for angling. It is important to remember that these can either be used to force the bait to sink faster or to cast the bait at a larger distance. Traditional sinkers are made from lead but, given the toxicity risk, these have been replaced by alternative materials, such as: steel, brass or tungsten.

The modern sinkers of today come in the most varied shapes and sizes; however, for bass fishing, it is recommended that you choose the heavier ones. You can choose for example split shots, as these are frequently used with live baits. Or, if you want, you can go with the rubber core sinkers. These have a characteristic groove in the center, this being the place where the line is held; the advantage of this sinker is related to the easy and comfortable maneuvering, plus there is no risk for nicking the line. Other types of sinkers recommended for bash fishing include: bell, pyramid, bank/reef, walking, egg shaped, cone sink and bullet shots.

The fishing rod is often used with the hook, line and sinker. The rod is used for the attachment of the fishing line, the hook being found at one of the ends. Today's modern rods are complex tools, being often provided with a fishing reel and a line guide. The materials used for the making of fishing rods include light bamboo, highly resistant carbon fiber and fiberglass. The one thing you have to remember about the fishing rod is that, the longer the rod, the bigger the casting distance is going to be. You can choose between different types of fishing rods, including: bait casting rod, fly rod and spin rod.

The fishing reel is found at one of the fishing rod, being used for the casting and luring in of the line. Anglers have the opportunity to choose between different types of fishing reels and they all know the advantages of such an equipment. When fishing for largemouth bass, the fishing reel allows you to launch the lure at a bigger distance. This means that you can approach the actual fish, without your physical presence spooking the fish away.

You will also need to include bait among your equipment, using either natural or artificial lures. Keep in mind that the largemouth bass is a fish that relies heavily on its instincts, having a horizontal stripe on its flanks that functions as an antenna. You need a good bait if you want to catch that fish. Among the most popular choices recommended for bass fishing, there are: stick baits, topwater poppers, grubs and spoons.

The stick baits are recommended because they easily attract the fish, providing a distraction on the water surface. The bass is easily attracted to the back-and-forth motion of the lure, which increases your chances of actually catching the fish. The topwater poppers create a rippling effect on the surface of the water, plus they make a specific sound when reeled. The grubs resemble the common worms but they are made from plastic; their versatility is the biggest advantage, as they can be used with any types of hooks. Plus, they come in all sort of sizes, styles and colors. The spoons are heavier in weight and they are ideal for bass fishing, especially in water with a lot of moss or other vegetation.

Apart from the equipment that was already mentioned, you can consider purchasing a bite indicator, which will be helpful in determining whether something is happening at the hook or not. You will also need a tackle box, in which to keep all the bait and other fishing accessories. The boat is also a big decision to make– however, it is recommended that you choose something simple, to get you on the water and nothing more. When you gather more experience, you can also switch to a more complex option.

As you will be spending a lot of time in the open outdoors and perhaps in the water, you will need to purchase specific fishing clothing. If you want to spend a lot of time in the water, it is recommended that you purchase fishing waders. Otherwise, you should stick with a comfortable T-shirt and shorts. A rain/windproof jacket should be considered for colder days. On the other hand, you should always wear a cap and sunglasses in order to protect yourself from the sun. Applying sunscreen with high SPF is also a good idea and you need to consider insect repellent, as mosquitoes love water. Choose footwear that is comfortable and dries out easily.

Chapter 8: The best techniques for bass fishing

The proper technique can greatly increase your chances for catching that first fish. With the passing of time, thanks to the constant practice, you will become more experienced and you will be able to try the most complex bass fishing techniques. In this chapter, you will find the best bass fishing techniques, recommended in particular for those who are just beginning to discover angling as a hobby. Be sure to try all of them out and see which one works the best.

Two of the most popular bass fishing techniques are represented by pitching and flipping. Both of these techniques are recommended for catching the largemouth bass, especially when there is a lot of vegetation in the water and you do not want to risk spooking the fish. Even though the techniques may seem the same, there are some differences between them. However, for both of these two techniques, you will need a rod of considerable length and a bait that is, preferably, soft. And, yes, you will need to practice a lot.

Pitching is a bass fishing technique recommended for beginners, as it is easier to try out. However, you must remember that it is not as precise as flipping. For successful pitching, you need to have enough line let out, so that it is even with the fishing reel. Keeping your reel open, you will need to lower the tip of the road in the direction of the water. Using your other hand, make sure that you grab hold of the bait and then pull on the fishing line, adding tension to it. One motion is enough to slingshot the bait in the direction of the bait. If the bass has landed, make sure that you close the reel quickly. Keep in mind that the largemouth bass is a fish that will fight to get off and an open reel is not a good idea.

As it was already mentioned, flipping is more precise than pitching, but it requires a little bit more experience. However, if you want to try the flipping technique, you need to start by letting out some fishing line and closing your reel. For the next step, make sure that you grab the line that is found between the reel and the first guide, pulling on the line afterwards. Raise the rod, so as you see the lure swinging. Tighten the line and wait for the bass to bite. The more you practice the flipping technique, the easier it will seem. As in other fields, practice makes perfect.

Another bass fishing technique is based on the usage of topwater lures. This technique is recommended for largemouth bass fish, as these are always hungry and moving actively underwater. The advantage of this technique is that the topwaterlures attract the attention of the fish, through a clever combination of sound and movement. The technique can be practiced in two ways. The first one requires that you pop the lure during the retrieval. The secret is that you take a pause every couple of seconds and then leave it slide through water. The bass will mistake the lure for a wounded fish, biting without hesitation. The second variant will require that you jiggle the tip of the road, retrieving the lure gradually— all of the movement is going to attract the attention of the bass, which guarantee the successful biting and catching.

The bass fishing technique that is based on the usage of crankbaits is also recommended for beginners. Crankbaits present a number of advantages, being indicated for waters of different depths and also for environments where there is a lot of vegetation, rocks or wooden logs. In order to attract the attention of the largemouth bass, you need to reel the lure fast and stop suddenly; this will allow for the lure to rise to the surface of the water. The next step will be to reel really fast again and then do the stopping movement. This will confuse the fish and it will make it easier to catch.

The spinner bait technique is also used for the catching of the largemouth bass but you have to remember that getting the bait on the hook is a little bit more complicated. Spinner baits are recommended to be used in environments with luxuriant vegetation, rocks or logs, just like crankbaits. The attraction of the fish can be obtained by the slow reeling, until the bait reaches the bottom of the water. As you feel it hitting the bottom, you reel it in again. You need to repeat these steps over and over again, always changing the pace of the reeling. This will make the bass confused and you will be able to catch it, without too much effort.

Chapter 9: Tips and tricks for successful bass fishing

In this chapter, you will find a wealth of information on how to fish for bass and especially for the largemouth variety. Read the tips and tricks that are presented here, as they will help you in your fishing adventure.

The first and most important thing that you should keep in mind that the best time to fish for largemouth bass is during the pre-spawn period. In case you are wondering when this period actually is, you should know that it starts in the spring. The water temperature starts to increase and the largemouth bass will move to the waters that are shallow, being interested in only two things: feeding and finding the best place to nest.

During the pre-spawn period, you will notice that the bass is quite active and interested in feeding. You will also see them getting quite close to the shoreline. So, if you want your fishing adventure to be a success, you need to consider this period. If you catch a large-sized bass, be sure to release it, as this is probably a female and it needs to complete the spawn process. Otherwise, you can interrupt the cycle of life for the bass and this is certainly not a responsible way to fish. The catch and release practice should always be respected.

As other species of fish, the bass has certain habits and it is quite useful to know them. For example, the largemouth bass is greatly influenced by the weather outside. If there is a lot of sun, the fish will look for shelter while, if it is cloudy, you will see it roaming more freely around. Why is this important to know? If there is a lot of sun, you can choose to fish in the areas where the bass would normally look for shelter. On the other hand, if it is cloudy, you have more chances of catching the bass, without too much effort.

Is there a right time in the day to fish for bass? The answer is clearly yes. In fact, there are two moments in the day when you have high chances for success. The first one is represented by the wee hours of the morning, just before the sun rises, while the second is represented by the last hours of the evening, just before the sun sets. There is one more thing that you should know about the habits of the largemouth bass– if it happens that the weather is cloudy or the water is muddy, there is a higher chance for the bass to choose the evening for feeding, coming to the shallower waters and near the shoreline. So, this means you have higher chances to catch your first, beautiful largemouth bass.

After you have chosen the location for your fishing adventure, it is time to do a little bit of research. Keep in mind that each body of water has its own map and this map can provide a wealth of useful information. It can be used to determine the depth of water in certain places and also to the precise identification of the places that the bass might prefer for shelter. With the passing of time, you can improve the map, marking the exact locations where the fish landed and the ones in which nothing happened. In this way, you can increase the chances of success, with each fishing experience and enjoy your adventure to the max.

At first, not having that much experience, you might not find the fishing experience so interesting. The truth is that fishing requires a lot of patient but the reward at the end, when that fish bites, makes it all worth it. The important thing is that you do not let your mind drift away and take your eyes of the line. There are many problems that can arise, with you thinking about other matters. In the majority of the cases, the fishing line can become frayed, as it comes into contact with stumps, rocks or even gravel. Sometimes, there are branches submerged in the water and these can harm the fishing line as well. You need to be careful and protect your fishing equipment from potential damage.

In choosing your first baits, you might be tempted to choose the ones that are bigger in size, believing that these will increase your chances of catching a fish. Well, things do not function exactly as you might expect and it is certain that the size of the bait does not influence the size of the bass you might catch. Instead of focusing on the size of the best, it might be for the best if you choose baits that are brightly colored, making both sound and movement. The trick is to also know how to use the bait, so that you attract the attention of the fish. Size really doesn't matter in this case.

If you want to maximize your chances of catching a largemouth bass, you need to use live bait. It might be a little bit more difficult at first but, as you will catch your first fish, you will see that it was worth the effort. Among the most popular choices for live bait, there are: worms, shiners, crayfish and frogs. The depth of the bait can be adjusted with the help of a slip bobber; in this way, you can cast your bait, without any effort or problem whatsoever.

The largemouth bass is the kind of fish that will come to the shore once it gets dark, as it was already mentioned. Even though you might be tempted to use a flashlight to spot the fish, refrain from such actions. The bass is extremely sensitive to light and you might end up losing what would have otherwise been a very nice catch. Also, do not hesitate to invest in top-quality fishing equipment– you might have to spend some money but your investment will pay off in terms of longevity.

Chapter 10: The practice of catch and release

Even though the practice of catch and release has existed since the 1950s, it was only recently that it started to be actively encouraged. The largemouth bass is an abundant specie at the moment and this is all due to the conservation efforts made through this practice. Both recreational and professional anglers encourage the practice of catch and release, being perceived as an act of conservation that ensures the continuity of these species.

If you want to be a responsible angler, you need to release the largemouth bass you have caught. You can do it immediately, unhooking it and making sure that it returns into the water, before any serious injuries have occurred or the fish is exhausted. Sometimes, the fish can be maintained in a live well for photos and measurement, but it will have to be returned into its natural habitat in the end.

There are many steps you can take in order to ensure responsible fishing, including when it comes to the equipment you are using. For example, the supporters of this practice encourage anglers to use barbless hooks, as these are known to facilitate the release process (reduced handling time due to the easy hook removal), reducing the risk of injuries.

As a beginner into the world of bass fishing, you always have to think about the purpose of this activity. You are not fishing to actually keep the fish but rather to enjoy the experience. The catch and release is the best thing you can do, in order to ensure that there will be health populations of fish in the future. This is even more valid for the larger fish, as these are breeding females, ensuring the continuity of the species. In only certain cases, you can consider keeping the smaller fish.

One of the main ideas behind this practice is the minimizing of the fight time. In order to achieve this objective, you need to choose the correct equipment for the fishing of the largemouth bass. By using adequate rods, reels and fishing lines for the bass species, you will decrease the fight time and thus protect the fish from injuries. You might not be aware of this fact but, the longer the fish will fight to escape from the hook, the more lactic acid is going to be produced inside the body. The buildup of lactic acid leads to the exhaustion of the fish, reducing its chances for survival.

Even though the usage of a thicker fishing line is not recommended because the largemouth bass might spot you easier, this is encouraged in order to protect the fish. The heavier or thicker fishing lines are indicated in the situation there is a lot of vegetation in the water or the temperature of the water has increased due to the water; by using this kind of fishing line, you will reduce the amount of stress placed on the fish.

The unhooking process can be quite complicated, especially if you don't have the right tools by your side. In order to protect the fish you have caught, you must use specific tools for its release. Among the most essential release tools that you need to carry with you during your fishing adventure, there are: spreaders for the jaws, bolt cutters (small-sized), hookouts and needle nose pliers. The usage of release tools becomes even more essential in case of larger fish.

In case you are not planning to photograph or measure the bass you have caught, you can use a special net in order to protect it. This special net will facilitate the unhooking process and it will reduce the stress placed on the fish. For the largemouth bass, the recommended choice is represented by the soft fiber knotless mesh. The main purpose of the net is to protect the slime layer that fish need in order to stay healthy.

In the situation that you have taken the bass out of the water in order to measure or photograph it, you need to keep it in a special well. Apart from that, you should avoid touching the bass with dry hands or place it on surfaces that are dry. Such actions will affect the protective layer of slime and will also contribute to the removal of scales. When fish are mishandled, they become more vulnerable to different infections of the skin, primarily caused by fungal microorganisms. In order to transfer them from the water to the well, make sure that your hands are wet or consider using a wet towel for such purposes.

You may have seen anglers who keep their catch in a vertical position, the bass being hanged by the jaw or the gills. As a responsible fisherman or angler, you should avoid keeping the fish in this position. Instead, you need to keep the largemouth bass in a horizontal position and support its body. By doing that, you will reduce the risk of injury to the internal organs, especially in the larger specimens. Another thing that you should avoid is gripping the fish by the eye sockets, as this will lead to the abrasion of the eyes and ultimately to blindness. When holding the fish for photos/measurement, you also need to take into consideration the placement of your hand. Avoid keeping your hand on the gills of the fish—instead, place it exactly under the jaw.

The fish can be measured in the water, using a special floating ruler or on board. However, if you decide to measure it on board, make sure that you wet the ruler before actually using it. In general, you should not keep the fish out of the water for more than 25 seconds, this being the recommended time for photos and measurement. Also, if you want to weigh the fish, avoiding using the scales in which the bass is hung by the jaw. Not only does this method of weighing damage the jaw or the gills but it may also damage the spine and the internal organs.

Once you are done with the measurement, release the fish gently in the water and know that you have taken the right decision. In the end, this is all responsible fishing is all about.

Chapter 11: What Is The Bass Fish?
Understanding Bass Fish.

The bass fish is one of the most commonly found fished in the world but is mostly fished in the US. These fish are fresh water fish and are generally found in abundance.

Let us answer a few questions about the same in order to give you a better picture of what these fish are and what bass fishing is all about.

Q: What is Bass fishing?

A: Bass fishing refers to the act of fishing for the bass fish. Bass fishing has been a tradition in many families for many years and these fish are some of the most sought after varieties. They are also consumed but are mostly considered as gamefish (recreational).

The most common type of gamefish is the Black bass, which is fished mainly for recreational purposes. They are said to be extremely tough to catch, which make them an ideal gamefish. The method used to fish these is known as "Angling", a term that was popularized by the fishing community in North America.

Q: Where are they from?

A: Although the very origins of the bass fish are not known or are under dispute, most bass fish can be found in the US, Europe and some parts of Asia like Japan and China. The art of catching Bass fish is said to have originated in Europe and was then rapidly part of the culture of the American fishing community.

The Europeans sought tips and tricks from the Americans and the Japanese and in turn, started to develop their own techniques of fishing.They are also exported to other countries but their main abode can be zeroed in on as the US.

Q: Where can they be fished from?

A: Most bass fish are found in any freshwater body and are scattered all over the country. Some of the best places in the US can be found in North America as that is supposed to be where most bass fish breed and reproduce. They are found in abundance and can be easily fished from any fresh water body.

During the civil war, several fishermen fled their homes in North America and settled in the eastern coast. They carried their bass with them and in turn, started to breed them in the western regions, with California being one of the main ports. And so the Northern and Western regions began to host a majority of the bass population in the world.

Q: What are their varieties?

A: The Bass fish have a lot of varieties and in fact, two types of species come under the bass species. One of them being the freshwater bass, and the other is the Marine bass fish. The black bass is a variety of fish that is extensively found in North America and has 6 sub categories of fish.

These categories include the Choctaw bass, the Guadalupe bass, the largemouth bass, the small mouth bass, the spotted bass and the centrarchidae.

Other forms of bass fish include the European sea bass, the striped bass and the white bass, all of which are found in the waters of Europe.

The Japanese sea bass and the black sea bass are found in the Asian waters.

Q: Are they only for sport?

A: No. Although bass are considered to be gamefish, they are also eaten in several parts of the world. They are low in fat and contain good amounts of omega 3 fatty acids. But one thing to be cautious about when consuming bass fish is that they need to be checked for mercury content.

Most bass fish can have high levels of mercury and depending on where you fish them from; they need to be checked for mercury levels. The European sea bass and the Japanese black bass are some of the most preferred types of fish and are even served at posh restaurants as being exotic fish varieties.

Q: Are there competitions for the same?

A: Yes. There are several competitions that are organized worldwide and several clubs where you can get membership. The act of fishing for sea bass began in the 1800's and by the turn of the 1900's several communities began to host competitions.

The Bass Anglers Sportsman Society, which was formed by the "Ray Scott" who is said to be the father of bass fishing, conducts an annual bass fishing competition called the Bassmaster Tournament Trail. It was first started in 1969 and every year, 50 of the best fishing folk compete in 12 events to win the big prize of $500,000.

Other events include the Walmart FLW tour, where the best fisher stands the chance of winning $1 million.

The third and best competition is the U.S. Open of bass fishing, which is held every year and the winner wins $500,000. Several Asian countries such as Korea and Japan and world countries such as Australia and South Africa also hold yearly bass fishing competitions.

Q: Are there seasons for bass fishing?

A: Most of these competitions are held in a particular season when bass fish are easy to catch and start to appear on the top water.

They do so to mate or lay eggs. These competitions are mostly held during midyear.

Q: Are there rules that govern bass fishing?

A: Most competitions have their own set of rules but the winner is usually judged by the size of the fish that he/ she catch and how fast they can catch. Apart from the length, its weight is also considered as a final deciding factor.

Q: Is there a way to free the fish?

A: Yes. If you are not interested in killing the fish for consumption you can release it back into the water. If you catch a fish and realize that it is not big enough or long enough to help you win then you can immediately release it back. You can hold on to the fish that is longest and biggest.

If you are catching bass fish for recreational purposes then you can release it back after you are done photographing it.

Q: Is bass fishing only for adults?

A: No. The act of fishing for bass fish can be performed by anybody and there is no age limit. Depending on how safe the water is and how safe it is for kids to go fishing, any young boy or girl can start training in bass hunting.

Chapter 12: Best Settings To Catch A Bass Fish

Now that we had a look at what the bass fishing is all about, let us look at the details of each type of fish and the best conditions that are suited for bass fish hunting.

Types of bass fish

Bass fish are of two kinds and are mostly found in the fresh waters of North America. Their original natural habitat is Eastern America. Their excessive breeding and farming led to their populations being scattered all over USA.

The main type of gamefish is the black sea bass, which is the prize that is to be hunted for most bass competitions.

These fish are extremely ideal as they are mostly available on the top waters. You can easily identify a black sea bass by looking at its color. The skin has to be black.The fish develops the dark color owing to extreme sun exposure and much like human skin tanning, fish also tan.

But one note of caution is that, you must not consume black sea bass as they will emit a very strong pungent taste.

Apart from these fish, you can also fish for the largemouth bass, the small-mouth bass and the striped bass when you use angling as a technique to fish for freshwater fish.

Just like how you have to have an ideal setting while hunting for other wild animals, you have to have an ideal setting when hunting for fish. Here, we look at:

Location

The best place to look for bass is in areas that have only little grass and have large rocks. These large rocks and other such stones are what sea bass like to hang around and more often than not, try and use them to hide behind. This technique is especially useful when fishing for black sea bass.

When fishing for largemouth bass, you have to drop your hook into shallower water that has more cover. These fish prefer extremely shallow water and will be present within a 3 or 4 inch depth. They also prefer smaller ponds that have a constant current running through them.

Time

On average, there is no particular time frame for sea bass to be available readily. Any time of the day will be fine as long as it is not too late or too early.

The best time to fish for sea bass is in the mornings. When it is sunny, you can find the black sea bass at about 4 to 6 inches depth. You will find the fattest fish in the afternoons as they will take some time to float to the top and look for their food. Mid-afternoon's around 2 pm are the best time to catch fat sea bass that will be quite heavy.

If you are looking for smaller bass then you can go at dusk to small ponds to look for small fish. These small fish are easy to catch as they will be attracted by any moving object and confuse it for food. In fact, dusk is the best time for you to practice.

Water conditions

The water should be fresh if you are looking for bass. Most bass prefer warm to medium water and also remain on the top warm surface.

Black sea bass will be mainly in warm water as they prefer warm water. All fish are cold blooded and so they will prefer to be in warm temperatures in order to be in warm conditions.

Some bass will also be present in cold water and you will have to put your hook in deeper to find them. They will mostly be inactive and you might have to use attractive bait for it. But remember, if the water is too hot then there will be lesser oxygen on the top surface and so these bass will avoid coming to the top. You might have to use a longer rod to push the bait and hook deeper into the water during such circumstances.

Apart from the level of the water, you might also have to check the currents. Most bass love mild currents and will be close to large rocks and other such obstructions as they will amplify the current.

Weather conditions

Most bass fish have the tendency of moving to waters that are warm. So in summer months, these fish will be on the top water and in the winter months, they will prefer water at medium depth. Depending on the season, you will have to choose the rod accordingly.

The best time to fish black sea bass is just after spawning. They prefer to mate and lay eggs in the months of fall and by end of fall, most sea bass are vulnerable.

Autumn is also a good time for these fish to be on the surface. They will be on the top surface and so it will be best for you to use a shallow water rod and line. Another good time to look for sea bass is just before a storm. Most fish can predict the weather and they will stay low. If you drop in bait, they will most definitely be attracted to it in fear of losing out on a source of food.

If you head out and fish for them just before a storm or rainfall then you are sure to catch a sea bass

Precautions

There are a few precautions that you must take before you go bass hunting. Especially during the summer months when the water will be extremely hot and so will the weather.

With hot weather, the fish will turn lazy and stay under the surface. The angler will have to spend that much more time to wait for these fish as they will prefer to not burn energy and stay affixed at one point.

Afternoons in summers are possibly the worst times for anglers to go fishing as these fish will not rise to the surface at all and the angler will have to wait in extreme heat and end up with no catch at all.

So it is extremely important for the angler to bear in mind the various ideal conditions that were mentioned before going fishing.

Chapter 13: Tips And Tricks For Catching Bass Fish

Now that we looked at the various conditions that will suit the bass fish, we must look at the various tips and tricks that professionals use in order to land the biggest, longest and best fish.

These tips and tricks are as follows.

Tips and tricks for bass fishing

1.   Understand their habits

It is always important to understand the habits of the bass fish. They will have certain characteristics that will allow you to understand where they will be present. They tend to follow a certain pattern. Just by observing their behavior, you will be able to surmise as to which the best part of the water is for you.

You can also set up a camera and observe which parts they swim in. You will then be successful in catching these fish and after you have your first catch, you will know which part is best for you to fish at.

2.   Understand the species

It is important for you to understand your species. The bass species is quite a popular one and you will find lots of information. You can have an in depth look into the species' behavior and how they will react to your bait.

You can look into the various characteristics of the fish and which part of the water will be the best for you to fish at. You must also decide on the variety of fish that you would like to hunt. You have to determine if it will be the black bass or any of the other type of bass.

3.   Get the timing right

It is not an understatement when I say that timing is everything when it comes to bass fishing. These fish can be extremely fast and also have erratic habitats.

As was mentioned in the right conditions section, you have to get your timing right when you go fishing. It all depends on how well you pick the time to go fishing and determine the best place to go fishing. You must also understand as to how long you have to spend during your trip in order to effectively have a catch.

4.   Understand the water body

Understanding the water body will be extremely important. You will have to thoroughly understand its various sections and observe the fish. You must get into the water and swim around a little to look at these fish.

By doing so, you can find out the exact time of the school of fish that will frequent the particular area and the time frame for them to arrive. Most bass fish follow a particular pattern and it will be easy for you to understand and predict the time and place where they will appear.

5.   Talk to experts

One of the best things to do when undergoing training to become a pro is to talk to some of the experts. The experts will give you some valuable advice and also let you in on some tips and tricks.

You will know what to expect when you go bass fishing and how to react to certain situations. If there are no experts around then you can ask some of the local fishermen. Fishermen are in fact, some of the best people to talk to as they will have understood the waters through and through. They will know exactly what is to be done to catch these fish.

6.   Look at them catching a bass

You can have a practical lesson with the expert or the local. Go with them on a fishing trip and look at what they do. They will allow you a glimpse of the best method to be adopted to catch the fish. They may let you in on a few of the ways in which you can successfully catch the bass fish. You will also understand the best time and place to fish at.

7.   Have the best equipment

One of the best aspects of bass fishing is to have the very best equipment. If you have cheap equipment, then you will have less success. It is important to have the best bait, the best fishing rod, the best line, the best hooks etc. they will determine the type of fish that you will end up catching.

Look for the second best equipment when you undergo training and the best equipment when you decide to take part in competitions. Remember, even if you are good at fishing, you will need good equipment to help you. You do not want your large bass to fall back into the water owing to a weak line or a substandard hook.

8.   Understand the casting styles

Casting styles refer to the process of casting the flexible rod into the water during the angling. The standard practice is to flick the rod over the head and flick it into the water as far as possible. There are also various other techniques, such as swinging the rod towards the side.

The casting style is important as it will determine the falling of the lure or bait into the water. It will also determine how deep the hook will lie. It is important to get the right angle and casting style and only regular practice will bring about perfection.

9.   Bait selecting

It is important to select the right kind of bait. The tackle shop personnel might recommend the best but you can also do a little research online. Most bass fish love bait that move rapidly. They like only those that have a fast movement and try and grab them out of fear of losing them.

You can either attach live bait or plastic ones. As per research findings, bass fish are most attracted to plastic or rubber worms that have rapid wriggly movement. You can also rub a few dead worms over plastic ones just to smell like live bait and use the wriggle movement to your advantage.

10.   Never give up!

When you are training to be a pro and wanting to compete professionally, it will seem like a very daunting task in the beginning but through regular practice and a strong determination, you will be able to turn extremely efficient in fishing.

You will start to garner confidence with every subsequent catch and also be able to catch many fish in a row. Do not give up and keep at it regularly.Do not be discouraged if you are not able to catch any initially, it will start to get better and in no time, you will find yourself competing with the best and maybe even beat them!

Chapter 14: Bass Fishing Box Contents

In order to be well prepared to catch the best bass fish, you have to be equipped with the best equipment.

The various equipment needed to be top class is paramount as you will have only a little time to make your catch and you will need the best equipment to do so.

1.   Fishing rod

Bass fishing requires a firm and strong rod. The idea is to find a rod that will bear the traction when you fling it before you cast it into the water. The rod that you choose for bass has to be a little flexible but not too much.

It must be aptly flexible and as per fishermen who hunt bass fish, the rod must be medium action flexible. The best way to determine the flexibility is by testing it yourself before buying. For assistance, the rod's flexibility will be mentioned on the rod's handle.

Another important aspect to consider while choosing a rod is to look at its compatibility with the reel that you are using. Your bass fishing casting rod will either be compatible with a spin cast or bait cast reel.

You have to also decide on the material that you would like to use. You can either choose traditional wood or settle for graphite or even fibreglass depending on your needs.

2.   Fishing line

You have to decide the best fishing line for yourself. Most bass fish will be extremely strong and tug at the line. You have to test the line first and see how tensile it is. You have to pull it enough to see how far it can go. You have to also check for its abrasion resistance and make sure that it does not snap when it rubs against itself. You can tie a knot at the end of the line to check if it will hold the hooks.

3.   Hooks

You have to look for sturdy hooks that will easily hold the bait and the fish. Depending on the type of bass, you will have to decide on the length of the hook. It might be small or big depending on whether it is a small-mouth bass or a large-mouth bass.4.   Pliers

You must buy a good pair of pliers that will allow you to adjust the hooks. You have to also use the pliers to twist the line and you need to use them to twist the hooks to help open it and allow you to add another one too.

5.   Bait

The bait is one of the most important parts of the tackle box. You have to make sure that you buy bait that will easily attract the fish. You can opt for either live bait or plastic or rubber ones. There are also the ones that are made of plastic but smell like real bait.

6.   Flashlight

Your carry kit must always have a flash-light. You will need it to look for fish at nights and also to look at your catch. You will also need it to attract help and use it as a signal to be used in case you are lost or stranded in a bad part of the water body.

7.   Super glue

The super glue will come in handy for you to fix an emergency break or an emergency snap. If you have no spare and are in an area that has lots of bass then you can use the glue to fix the break or snap.But be sure to carry a lighter along as you will have to heat the glue to make it more potent.

8.   Wrench

The wrench will come in handy in doing several things including opening the reel covers.

9.   First aid kit

You will have to keep a first aid kit handy, you should have one as it will help you in case of an emergency. There are several things that might cause you injury including the rod and the line. You will need immediate medical attention and only a first aid box will help you.

10.   Spares

Carry a spare for all your equipment including fishing rods, fishing lines, hooks etc. you can easily replace anything that gets damaged. Also have a spare flash-light.

Tackle

Opinions vary between bass fisherman about what equipment to use for jig fishing. My choice for jig and worm fishing is a 7'2" Shimano jig and worm rod, medium heavy with a fast tip.

I like this rod because it has enough backbone to pull the bass out of the thick stuff. It also has a sensitive enough tip so you can feel what is going on at the other end of the line.

For a reel, I like Shimano spinning reels. They have been my favorites since they started making them. I love the quick-fire reels because I love the quickfire trigger.I love the ability of one-handed casting with spinning gear. Once you use it for a while; it is so quick and easy.

I also prefer to fish jigs and worms on spinning gear instead of baitcasting gear, I like the feel of the lure better.The exception is swim jigs. I prefer to fish the faster baits, swim jigs, spinners, and crankbaits on baitcasting gear.

I carry four rods with me, so I am ready, three baitcasting, one with a spinner tied on and one with a crankbait tied on, and one with a Silver minnow or swim jig.The other one is the spinning rod with a worm or a jig.

As far as line goes. I use fluorocarbon on my spinning rig most of the time. The fluorocarbon does not have the memory coiling that happens with mono. I use braid on all my baitcasters. I like braid for the strength and for the thinner size, and no memory in the line. The strength of the braid is amazing.

My wife caught a rock in the river, I wrapped the line around my arm, with my jacket on and started walking until it came loose. I straightened out the hook. The line did not break.

The tackle you choose is more about what you like and what you feel comfortable with. There is nothing wrong with good quality monofilament line. I used trilene xt for 30 years and never had a problem with it. Your choice of rods, reels, and line has less to do with catching fish. Knowledge and confidence are much more important. If you like a set up, and you feel more comfortable fishing it, that will help you catch more bass.

Jig Color

For jig color, there is a lot of discussion about what colors are better, or if it even matters at all. Some fishermen do not think color makes much difference. Some think it makes a big difference. The ability to see color in water changes a lot as you go deeper, depending on the colors.

Color makes a difference. However, size and presentation, and if it looks like the bass choice of food are more important than color.

There are hundreds of colors and color combinations you can pick from. It is not as bad as going to pick out paint colors, but close.There are some that seem to be better than others. The key is not to choose colors you think look cool. It is easy to fall for that trap.

Many lure manufacturers make lures to attract fisherman and fish. You do not need every possible color of the spectrum. I am guilty of getting sucked into what looks cool. I have several lures that appeal to me by looks, not necessarily what the fish want.

There have been a few unofficial, unscientific studies done. They are asking fishermen to tell them what the best color they have found for jigs.

The top colors submitted are.

- Black Blue

- Black, blue flash

- Black, brown crawfish

- Olive pumpkin

- Green pumpkin

- Brown purple

- PBJ flash

- Peanut Butter Jelly

There are more color combinations that catch Bass. Many have caught Bass for thousands of anglers. These seem to have been the best color combinations for many years.

Most fishermen know bass love skirted jigs. There are now many types of skirt material. I like the newer silicone or live rubber ones. The reason Jigs work so well is because jigs look like crayfish. Crayfish are a preferred food source for bass in lakes from north to south.

I have found from experience that the above colors cover most of what I have had success with. Everyone has used black and blue with success. One of my other favorites is a brown, orange skirt, looks like the food, looks like a crawfish.

It depends a lot on what the forage fish is in that body of water. I would recommend starting with black and blue or black and brown. After that I would try a brown and orange, or a mix of green and black or green and brown.

These are general guidelines that seem to produce well.

● Shallow and dark water. The best colors seem to be combinations of black and blues. Black and reds, June bug and other bluegill colored, darker colored skirts.

• Deeper clear water impoundments. The browns and brown purple and the PBJ combinations seem to produce best.

• In areas of shallow clearer weedier water. The greens, and green pumpkin, and olive watermelon combinations seem to produce best.

Here is another general pattern. Largemouth go more for the black based colors. While Smallmouth bass go more for the brown based colors.

My favorite colors for largemouth are the brown, orange color, and the black and blue colors. I prefer green pumpkin and the PB and J in shallow weedy clear water. Keep an open mind on color, when nothing is working, try something different. It may be the trigger to turn them on.

General Tips

Denny Brauer said about jigs. "It is the most versatile bait in fishing." Brauer also says, "One of the main reasons I use jigs is because I like to catch big fish. I don't know of any other bait out there that appeals more to quality fish than a jig does."

He said, "jigs penetrate the heavy cover better than other lures. "They also hook and hold a higher percentage of fish."

There are a thousand different jigs you can get. They vary in size, weight, head shape, color, skirt type, skirt size, hook style. They also can have a weed guard or no weed guard, long skirts, short skirts, trailer, or no trailer, etc.

Here are general tips to remember when jig fishing.

● Jig fishing needs concentration: you must pay attention to what is going on below the surface.

● Fish jigs slow most of the time, slower when water is cold.

● Largemouth Bass prefer larger jigs than smallmouth bass.

● Jigs are great night fishing lures.

The most important thing to consider in jigs is the size. The size is critical to catching the most fish. If you want to catch bigger fish, stay with the bigger jigs, if you want to catch more fish, drop a size.

This is a general rule. I have caught some huge bass on small jigs, but the normal is bigger jig, bigger bass.Trailers count as to the size. If you add a big trailer, you have a bigger jig.

You want the jig to be heavy enough to get the jig down to where you want it in the water, but not heavier than what it needs to be. Like a worm, the slow dropping bait will attract more fish than a heavy jig sinking to the bottom like a rock.

I have caught most of my bass on jigs in the 1/4 and 3/8 oz. size. In the northern lakes of Minnesota and Wisconsin where I do most of my fishing, these sizes have been the best for me. Unless your Flippin into thick weeds, I would not go bigger than ⅜ most times. If you want a bigger jig, add a bigger plastic trailer to the jig or a bigger skirt.

Here are the recommended weights of jigs for specific types of fish.

Panfish and Crappies 1/32, 1/16, 1/8 oz.

Trout and Salmon 1/16, 1/8, 1/4 oz.

Walleyes and Bass 1/16, 1/8, 1/4, 3/8, 1/2 oz.

Northern Pike and Muskies 3/4, 1, 1 ¼, 1 1/2 oz.

Lake Trout and Stripers ¾, 1, 1 ½, 2 oz.

For big bass and situations where weeds are thick, ¾ and 1 oz jigs or even bigger for bass are not uncommon.

How to fish Jigs

A jig is most of the time a drop bait. You cast the jig to the spot, engage the reel or not, and let it drop to the bottom on a tight line or on a slackline.Let it sit for a minute or longer, then take up the slack and jiggle it around once or twice.

If the jig is not hit, move the jig up and toward you. Then let it drop back to the bottom. Repeat the wait and jiggle, repeat it over again a couple more times. If no takers bring it back and try a different spot.

Many strikes will come on the initial drop. It may only feel like a stop, or a slight twitch; you may feel it move away. If you feel any of these things, take up the slack and use a sweeping motion to set the hook.

One key with jigs. Like with most lures in shallow water, is you want the jig to enter the water with as little noise as possible. Learn how to cast with the jig close to the water. You want it to hit so it comes in with as little splash and noise as you can. This is important in not scaring the fish away.

Learn what the jig feels like when it is lying on the bottom, think about what it is doing. When you feel something different than when it is lying there alone, set the hook. Many bass hits are a tap or a slight move. They do not hit it like a fast-moving lure, most hits are very subtle.

If you have a weed guard on the jig, set it more like you would a Texas rigged worm.Set it harder to draw the hook past the weed guard and into the fish's mouth.

Do not be afraid to let the jig sit still for longer than you may think. Then shake it once or twice without moving it toward you. Do not be afraid to set the hook hard.

Seasonal

Spring

In the spring, you want to go with slow falling lighter jigs. The bass are sluggish and not moving fast because of the cold water. I like to use an 1/8 or ¼ oz. jig with a grub trailer.

One of my all-time favorites in colder water is a Roadrunner jig. It has a grub trailer with a small spinner on the bottom side. They work well for bass in colder water.

A jig with a crayfish trailer is also good in colder water. You should cast and let the jig drop to the bottom. Then reel up the slack and give it a twitch to make it shake like a dying fish.

As the water warms up, you can move the jig faster and even hop it along the bottom.

When fishing docks in cold water, let it sit after the cast for up to a minute or even longer. You will startle the fish if a jig drops into the water. If the jig lands a couple of inches away from the fish, you need to give them time to come and investigate. Once their initial shock from the lure landing goes away, they will check it out.

Bass will move into the shallows in the spring. When they do this, points and drop offs are one of the key places to find them with slow fished jigs. Look for points and drop offs with any weeds, this is the first cover they will go to as the weeds grow.

In cold water, a drag and shake retrieve works well.Let the jig drop to the bottom, let it sit, drag it a few inches and give it a shake, then let it sit again, and repeat.

Summer

In the summer, jigs are great for fishing docks and other structure and thicker weeds. You can use bigger jigs in the summer. Because the bait fish they eat are larger, that is what they are looking for, so go bigger with your baits.

Jigs are great dock baits year-round. I like to come up to a dock and fish across the front, hop the jig along the front of the dock. Then move to where you can cast down one side and hop it out, next fish down the other side and hop it back.

If the dock is a big dock, throw the jig up under the dock. Most of the docks in the northern states are only 4 feet wide, because they cannot survive ice. They must come out in the fall and be put back in the spring.

If you are fishing heavy weeds, you need to pick a jig that is big enough to get through the mat of weeds. Once through the top it can then get to the bottom.Go with the lightest jig you can, that will get through the weed matt.

Once the jig goes through the mat, let it drop straight to the bottom. If it does not get hit, give it a little hop, if still no hit, pull it out and try a different spot.

This is a Flippin technique; you find the holes and drop the jig in the holes, then go on to the next hole.

Fall and winter

As the water temp drops, jigs still work well. You need to change your technique. You need to fish slower. Focus on shorelines with steep drop-offs and deeper coves. Furthermore, look for long points that drop off into deeper water.

Look for flooded trees and any remaining weeds; make sure you fish any docks that are still in the water.

Look for areas that have warmer water. If you can find an area that is 5 to 10 degrees warmer, it can make a huge difference.

Start with the lightest possible jig for the conditions. You want to feel what the jig is doing; a good starting point is ¼ to 3/8 oz.

Head Styles

There are tons of jig heads and variations of jig head styles. I will not attempt to list them all.This is a short breakdown of the ones I use and have found to be the most effective jigs for catching bass.

There are many different head styles for jigs. The variety of shapes and styles do different things for different situations. Jig head shapes are oval, round, football, stand up, skipping head, swim jigs heads, and many slight variations of those. There are variations of these that are different, but they are like these shapes.

Many bass jigs also have a weed guard, that help you fish in heavy cover and get fewer snags.

The football head jigs are one of the best to use on rocky bottoms without getting hung up. Bullet or oval or longer head jigs work best in weedy areas. The heads slide through the weeds best because they have no corners to get hung up.

Arky style jig heads are one of my favorites. They are great for Flippin into heavy weeds. Also dragging through wood and other structure. Football jigs work best in rocks and Arky heads will work best almost everywhere else. I would classify it as a long oval style head, and it also stands up well.

Another big jig for me in heavy cover is the Booyah Boo Jig. They come in lots of good colors, and have a heavy weed guard and a nice shaped head for pulling through weeds.

Nutech jigs are one of my new favorites. The jig at the beginning that I caught that nice fish on is a Nu tech jig. These are a great stand-up jig. They are a type of football jig. Basically, I use two main types of jigs, a stand up for a slow presentation, and a swim jig type head for quicker presentation where more weeds are involved.

Another one of my favorite jigs is the Roadrunner jig. They have a small spinner on the underside of the jig. They also have an unusual head shape that makes them snag resistant.

They are a great Crappie jig, but in the bigger models with a nice curly tail trailer on them, they are a killer bass lure. I have had great results fishing docks with roadrunner jigs.

The bigger ones are not as easy to find. But Bass Pro carries the ¼ oz size, and so does Cabela's, or you can get them from Blakemore.

Skirts

Most skirts are live rubber or silicone. Some have newer types of plastic. There are still skirts made from animal hair and types of marabou. They come in many colors, solids, and patterns.

The various skirt materials will make the jig look different. When the jig is sitting still or moving. Some fishermen think they look more lifelike than others. It is a subtle difference, and under tough conditions, it may change the way it works.

Matching the colors to the baitfish the bass are eating in the lake is still the key to getting the most bites. Adding a trailer can give you an advantage. Adding the extra bulk to the jig and adding a variation in color and attraction can also work.

Use a trailer that enhances or matches the jig color. You can use pork or plastic; pork will dry out, so they are not used often anymore. The soft plastic is much easier to use. Plastic can last for a long time, and not get hard like pork.

It is not a skirt, but it is effective under some conditions. I am talking about hair jigs. They are not used much for Bass fishing, but they can be fantastic in cold water that is clear.

Again, you want to match the jig to look like the forage the Bass are eating, and you want to fish them slow. For hair jigs, you also want to use small jigs, up to 3/8 oz.

The best colors are:

• Black -- Looks like a leach

• Brown -- Looks like a crawfish

• White -- Looks like minnows or shad

• Chartreuse -- Looks like perch, or sunfish.

• Smoke Gray -- Looks like most minnows.

The way to fish these jigs is to drag them along the bottom, do not hop or bounce them, drag them in the mud or sand. The jig is to imitate larva and small baby creatures.

Places to fish Jigs

Weeds

In many articles, you will read people saying they use certain lures when fishing grass. They mean weeds not just grass only. Jigs can be great to fish in all kinds of weeds, from thick Hydrilla to sparse scattered weeds.

They are the only lure you can use for the super thick stuff.Dropping the jig into holes in the weeds can catch lots of Bass. It is called Flippin.

If the vegetation is not as heavy, you can use swim jigs to fish over the top of and through the weeds.

When you fish in deeper weed beds, fish the jig on points or v's in the weed beds and outside edges. Bass focus on edges so they can ambush their prey easier. Hit the outside edges first. Then look for the inside edges that have something different.

Any other structure in the weeds can also be a perfect spot. A log or post or a dock are all prime locations. Even the shade from an overhanging tree or a boat can be a structure to the fish. Because it has defined edges and offers shade, the bass will relate to it.

If you are fishing a river or anywhere there is current. Look for something blocking the flow. A log or a rock rip rap. Then look for the Bass to sit on the back side of the object facing the current flow waiting for food to come to them.

Deep Water

If you are fishing deep water structure with a jig, use a medium size jig. Fish with a swimming retrieve, with a bouncing motion by pumping the rod tip up and down and pause occasionally. Cast the jig past the spot and let it sink to the desired depth. Once it is on the bottom, use the swimming retrieve through the structure.

Docks

I always fish docks with jigs. It is the best lure there is for covering all the prime places under and around a dock.I fish spinnerbaits and crankbaits and worms around docks as well. But my first choice is a swim jig, then a bottom finesse jig.

My favorite colder water dock jig is a black or a white roadrunner jig. Work it along the front first, then along both sides. Then if you can, get it under the dock and hit the dock posts when retrieving the jig. As the water warms up, go to a bigger swim jig. I like a white swim jig with a white twin tail trailer. Fish it like a spinnerbait just under the surface. Fish across the front and down each side. then go under if you can.

When you go to the finesse jig, try the sit, and wait technique first, then try fishing with a pumping motion.If no bites, try hopping it along the bottom.Often, the slower presentation will work better and catch more fish.

Shooting docks is a cool technique I discovered a couple years ago from a YouTube video. It is a crappie technique that will catch lots of bass. It is cool and lets you get under the docks. Works best on wide docks.Check out this video and see the technique.Let me know if you have tried it, it is amazingly effective for getting under docks. This technique also lets the lure hit the surface quietly and with little splash.

When you are fishing the deeper front side of the dock, cast past and retrieve it up to the dock. Then work it past the dock.When you are fishing the sides and throwing into the shallow water, let the jig sit. Let it sit after the cast on the bottom for up to a minute or two before you start your retrieve.

When the jig hits in a few inches of water, letting the fish get over the initial scare will help you catch a lot more Bass. If you find a dock with wooden dock poles, fish it hard. Wood pole docks are best for bass. Wood docks are better because the algae that grows on the wood attract minnows. The minnows attract bigger fish which attract the bass.Steel poles are second best; aluminum is the least desirous, but still do not pass them up.

Flippin

There is not much to say about Flippin, the technique is simple. it is not easy; it is the hardest technique there is to master. You find a spot, either a hole in the weed mat, or a spot in the submerged trees.

Use a heavy enough jig to get through the cover and get to the bottom. Let the jig drop all the way to the bottom before you move it.Do not even put any tension on the line until it gets to the bottom.

Hop the jig up and down twice. Then let it sit still, do this again, then pull it out of the hole and drop it in another hole in the weed mat.

It is simple on the surface, but you must be precise with where you drop the jig. You will also struggle to pull fighting bass out of thick weeds they want to tangle up in. It is difficult to do well.

You need to use a stout rod and heavy line for Flippin. When you hook a nice bass in the heavy weeds, you do not want to go in after them. You need to pull them out of the weeds before they get tangled in the weeds.

The arky style jig heads are my favorite for Flippin. Most styles of jigs that are not round will work good for Flippin. You want to pull the jig through the weeds, with or without a bass on the end of the line.

Grubs

Grubs are great for jig fishing; you can use any style of jig head with any size and color of grub body and use it as a swim jig or a bottom bouncing jig. You can rig it Texas style to swim through weeds or use it on a jig head with a weed guard to fish it in timber or weeds.

Grubs are also great to rig with a Carolina rig setup.

Here is a great video from Bass Resources that will show you the best ways to rig grubs.

Tube Jigs

When tube jigs first came out in the mid 80's as a Gitzit jig, they seemed like a fad. They were so different and flashy. They appeared to be trying to appeal to the fisherman, instead of the fish. The amazing thing about these funny looking flashy jigs is that they catch Bass, and lots of them.

Tube jigs are a big deal now; they are up there with the most fished jigs there are. Average fisherman and many pros use them. Tube jigs were made to slide a long slim headed jig into the tube and push the hook eye through the tube.You were then ready to fish them as a finesse jig or a swimming jig.

Since the beginning, many ways to rig them have become popular and used by many fishermen. Although the weighted head inside the tube is by far still the most popular. The popularity continues because it is effective and catches bass.

Fishermen now rig them every way you can think of. They add rattles, and scents, and fish them through and around every type of structure there is. They are one of the most versatile jigs there is.

How far you push the head into the tube affects the action of the jig. If you push it in all the way to the end, the jig will fall faster and spin less. If you want the jig to fall slower and spin as it falls, do not push it all the way to the end of the tube. Stop it back and experiment with how the jig works.

The tube jig is great for fishing under docks. It is the best jig there is for shooting under docks like the video in the dock fishing section above shows you how to do.

Another cool thing you can do is to soak cotton balls in scent and pull off a small piece. Shove the piece of scented cotton into the tube to give off scent for many casts as it comes out of the cotton ball.

Also, if you put a small piece of alka seltzer into the tube, it gives off bubbles that also attracts fish.

Another tip is if you cut off the end of the tube and use it as a skirt for a spinnerbait, or a skirt for a jig.

Ways to rig a tube jig

• Rig it Texas style, like a worm, you can leave the hook point embedded into the inside of the opposite side of the tube.

• You can also push it through the opposite side of the tube and slide it up under the outside skin.

• You can also point the hook point, so it faces down. On the outside of the opposite side of the tube so it will not catch on anything.

• It works great as a weightless worm type rig. Put the hook eye inside the tube and the point on into the opposite side to be weedless. The extra weight of the bigger body of plastic makes it fall nice and slow like a weightless worm.

• A Carolina rigged tube is a great way to fish where you would fish a Carolina rigged worm. Here is a video on how to tie a Carolina rig.

Tubes are bulky and will catch weeds. They are not great for real thick weeds you need to pull the jig through. They work great for Flippin into pockets, as you would other jigs.

Tubes are one of the most versatile lures.You can catch everything from crappies and perch, to bass to stripers. They are also effective on many kinds of saltwater fish.

You can use your imagination about how you can fish a tube. Try anything you can think of it may catch fish; it may be the next latest thing.

Here is another great video to watch that will show you some alternate ways to rig a tube jig.

If you have not fished tube jigs, get some and try them, you will soon wonder why you have not tried them before.

Swim Jigs

Swim jigs are one of the most popular type of jig now. they are also very versatile. You can use swim jigs for almost any type of fishing and in most types of cover.

Swim jigs are easy to fish. Fishing a swim jig is like fishing a spinnerbait without the spinner. All the same techniques you use for spinnerbait fishing will work with swim jigs.

This is the easiest artificial lure you can fish. Most times they work best by casting and using a steady retrieve back to the boat.Use a ¼ to 3/8 oz jig head, a skinny to fatter tapered jig works best for swim jigs.

There are special jig heads that have a different placement of the jig eye. The eye on top gives it the right action to make the jig swim in a way that attracts fish. Other head styles will do the job also, but the swimming jig heads work best.

You want to have a smaller weed guard on a swim jig than you would have on a Flippin jig. Swim jigs come with fewer fiber pieces on the weed guard. If you use a non-swim jig head for a swim jig, cut down the weed guard so it is not so thick.

When you set the hook with a swim jig, the most effective way is to use a sweeping action. This set will pull the hook into the side of the fish's mouth and you will hook more fish.

This past winter I bought over 20 different brands of swim jig heads. They are similar but are all a bit different. I have tried many of them now and I like several of them. I have made several of my own special swim jigs from different heads.

I think my favorite so far is The Davis Baits Elite Swim Jig, I use a zoom super hog trailer or a sweet beaver trailer.

Here is a good video that will show you some excellent tweaks to get the most out of your swim jig fishing.

Trailers

Trailers for jigs always bring up varying opinions about what type and why you should use them.

I would say most of the time trailers are good if you are trying to make the jig perform a different way. If you want it to look bigger, or if you want it to fall slower, trailers are the best way to do that. If you want to impart more action into the jig, trailers are great. If you want to add a different color to the jig, trailers will do that.

If you want the jig to be the opposite of any of these things, do not use a trailer.

There are also several types of trailers you can use. I know no one who uses pork anymore; I have not for many years. I use either a plastic crawfish trailer or a grub with a twister tail.

You can use varying colors and sizes depending on what you want the effect to be.

The Basics Of Bass Fishing – An Overview

Most, if no longer all of the so-referred to as 'insider' secrets and techniques, suggestions and stories to inform of huge hauls of Bass, all revolve, around a very easy basic rule – understanding the fish, (their life-cycles, feeding alternatives, conduct and patterns, dependancy and menu of choice, their nature, their relationship with the wider eco-system and position at the meals-chain, timing it right. Also heeding your environment, your device (gear), having the recognise how and basics beneath your belt and subsequently optimizing (each!) possibility…

In impact, you're going about, growing the maximum favorable angling procedure and final results you can muster!

Bass fishing is a passion, a technology and an art form upon itself. It appeals to young and old, draws anglers from all walks of lifestyles and each sides of the professional and beginner spectrum.

One key to bass fishing is, what we are able to effortlessly consult with as, 'predictable behavior'. Habits, patterns, lifestyles cycles, the herbal rhythm that is lifestyles and nature – additionally applies to fish. This method that Bass exist inside this natural fact. If you can capitalize on understanding it better, you may increase your probabilities of a hit hooks/bites.

Seeking defensive cowl, foraging among rocks, stumps, weeds, at instances on the prowl looking for prey, other times simply 'lunching' round casually, all seem to be part of The Bass feeding rituals and repertoire. Taking benefit and considering this while starting out and on every occasion casting, will benefit you significantly.

Another is "aggressive benefit", The Bass has an "airtight sac" (respiratory bladder), this is inflatable, which enables it to swim and thrive at special stages. A powerful tail enables with pace, agility and maneuverability. It can attain top notch depths.

Other factors like water readability, time of day, subdued sunlight, water displacement and vibration sensing, noise sensitivity, all upload to this fish' foxy and ensuring which you scrutinize those clues, will growth your odds of hooking your subsequent large one.

Unlocking as an example how The Bass senses and prefers colour and coloration in the moment, can continually additionally assist anglers boom their effectiveness. The desire and sort of lure, hues and movement, bait etc. Can all contribute meaningfully in your tries.

Where the fish are... each person could have a solution, or at the least their opinion/experience on what/in which/when, even technological know-how. Nevertheless, from time to time it is as simple as understanding the habitat and people that stay and thrive in it, to higher interact with and revel in fishing in it – a form of exploring the depths, so to speak.

For instance:

the temperature of the water and to be had oxygen, dictate transferring patterns and disbursement of fish species. Feeding conduct and preferences are wonderful, falling more at the "searching alive" or stay bait.

Some quote smallmouth bass, as showing choice for crawfish and the use of that as a 'sign' of in which those critters might be discovered, on the hunt for his or her favourite snack! Looking at belly content material of fishyou have got caught and kept (not part of the trap and release protocol/necessities), keep hidden clues about meals of preference – whitefish, crawfish and others.

Having self-self assurance, aptitude AND the right mind-set when fishing for Bass is crucial. In this warfare to outwit your opponent, you will want every device and trick at your disposal to make a successful capture. Never get discouraged, sense crushed or worse stop for the yield has been slim to none in any respect – the ones days occur to each angler. Nature beats to its personal drum, you need to discover and enjoy the rhythm you are so intricately part of.

Practice makes perfect – there is no silver bullet, quick-fish method for $9. Ninety nine, that can guarantee you bites and greater bass all the time, every time. It DOES take hard work and commitment, staying power and rigor from the angler.

There is greater than ordinary at stake and play here. Some days may be predictably better than others. No depend what the conditions, procedure and outcome, on the day, put all of it all the way down to experience and classes found out. Log and research,percentage and develop, inyour own information, confidence and toolkit, as an avid bass angler.

Another key trick, is without a doubt NO TRICK AT ALL – we name it an "obtained ability". It takes extra of that tough work we referred to before! Exact, fixed casting, requires goal-precision practice, enhancing your ability to vicinity the trap exactly in which you would need it to be – allow us to call it 'hitting the mark'.

Thisis any other essential tactic and method you could practice in the park or your dwelling room – attempt the use of plugs and get higher every time at continually hittingyour 'target' (and nothing else we are hoping!).

Becoming and being a proactive player within the context and environment (and process), you're in,understanding while to move on, alternate some thing and or quit for the time-being (suspending the quest or resting whilst required, making plans your method for the following journey out), is what it's miles all approximately as nicely!

Habitual creatures of consolation, The Bass (as a species), aren't so much one-of-a-kind than modern-day man. Bearing this in mind will help you too as an angler. We like what we adore, when and the way we find it irresistible and commonly need it on time, while it's miles there and equipped, be secure, enjoy existence and we crave comfort – meals, refuge and properly-being!

Does this sound loads specific from our very own desires and necessities? Not surely! Well, that is one way of leveling the gambling subject. Understanding the simple necessities and niceties for those watery"creatures", holds clues and benefit, for any and every angler.

Stimulus, pattern, habitual, habit – predictors and hints – the ace up your sleeve whilst nothing else works!Learn and develop capabilities, to 'study' (quick at a glance, take a look at and make a judgment), understand instinctively what is going to come occur, subsequent and why – discern out the pattern, stay with it and exploit it on your gain and angling fulfillment. Meet the Bass where they may be, in what they do, cater to their wishes and you may be surprised at what meets you in the waters beneath!

Familiarity with the Bass' favourite places to loaf around is critical to success: Bottoms, stumps, bushes , logs, weeds and plants, contours, structures, tour-routes, creeks, shallows/deeper passages, coves, channels,bluffs, banks and shores – all can be repetitive clues on ordinary, predictable behavior of the bass.

Most of the 'professionals' occurred their know-how thru studying, analyzing conduct of their catch, in very similar style than what you're task. Every time you get to understand your fishy pals a bit better, till you realize instinctively wherein they'll be and in which their favourite spots are.

Knowing and going where the fish are becomes demystified, but even more interesting,for it's far now extra than a slump or random hazard — it's far a deliberate stumble upon where the watery predator, hunter par excellence, becomes the hunted!

Tools Of The Trade: Tackle, Boats, Accessories, Lures And Baits (All About Plastics, Spinners, Crank And Others- Top-Water And Specialty Lures)

Having the right gadget, knowing how to best use it, when and the way, (additionally how no longer to apply it and what it isn't always suitable for), can all assist you to your bass fishing adventure.

The fundamentals regarding rods, reels, line, hooks, weights, bobbers, sinkers, lures, sensors and other system (hats, vests, nets, scents, scissors etc.), gives you an appreciation for having the proper tools for the assignment(s) at hand.

As a exceedingly participatory and engaging recreation, Bass fishing is absolutely almost unprecedented within the giant quantity of styles and gear to apply. From quiet streams, tranquil lakes to open sea and dashing rivers – there may be something for anyone.

If you are seeking out short guidelines on the proper device, most acceptable on your cause and the techniques to master to capture bass in any conditions, may this next segment enlighten and inspire you, as you delve right into the 'utilities of the fishing alternate'. Some equipment of the bass fishing exchange, we will be focusing on are:

☐ Rods, Reels, Lines and Hooks

☐ Tackle: Lures and Bait– live – synthetic and, or, BUT YET...

Limited area does no longer permit huge comparative factors or ramblings on the merit of a few tools above certain others. These debates are widely known and well posted in present literature.

We take a greater practical technique and have a look at what you'll really need to hook your subsequent huge one, besides random risk and good fortune! We want to factor out that choosing the right system way quite a few distinctive element to one-of-a-kind people.

Each angler has his/her personal interpretation of what that means, varying talent stage, physical traits and strengths/weaknesses, so we can no longer profess understanding what is proper for you. What we do provide are mere pointers on which tools will stack the odds to your prefer and assist you experience making ready, rigging, baiting/hooking, retrieving and landing YOUR next BIG ONE! Ensuring this is does no longer be a part of the droves of 'the ones that were given away'!

Even as you explore your surroundings and the surprise of fish species and their lifestyles cycles, patterns and behavior, experimenting, hands-on with your gadget and what's available to anglers nowadays, is a part of the exciting world of Bass fishing.

From fish-finders, temperature gauges, sensors and extra advanced technologies, to the artwork of preparing your strains and hooks, deciding on the lures/bait maximum suitable on your condition and reason and more, adds to the pleasure and enjoyment of the pastime.

Preparing your self with information on those, will improve your confidence and working towards frequently, pays off ultimately as your knowledge, exposure and angling mastery grows.

When it involves device, the opinions are many and a long way among. Your situation, condition, purpose and goal will all determine into the final preference (oh, yes and don't forget the ever-gift price range and affordability)!

Spinning or bait casting with artificial lures, fly-fishing, trolling with stay-baits, are all alternatives to be had to you, with specialist tools reachable to help you're making the most of it. Typically a 5.5 to 7 toes rod (spinning or bait casting), with an identical reel with six to ten pound line, fast taper, unmarried action reel might serve you properly. Weed-much less hooks are a lifesaver in very dense cover or weeds.

Angling techniques and address keep refining, developing and nearly takes on a lifestyles of its own for each angler. There isn't always certainly a one-size-fits-all method.

This personalised relationship with your equipment, might mean a simple rod to begin with and then including a couple in your special tours and expeditions – your Bass journey has simply started. Modern address and strategies, conventional or revolutionary, era-pushed and enabled – some thing your fancy or preference – there is something for each flavor and budget.

It is an historic recreation, pursued by using many, with echoes of early hunters and anglers residing off the land. Getting in touch with that timeline thru hands-on interest, like bass fishing could be very worthwhile. Most beginners is probably beaten via the choice of equipment available available on the market these days. Knowing what to choose/purchase, how and when to (best)observe, use it efficiently, to maximize your probabilities of catching your next big one is key.

Good high-quality address is important – it needs to be ok for some thing nature throws your way. You will want to build your arsenal of understanding and equipment over the years, to reply first-rate to a number of the demanding situations at hand.

Good suitable baits and lures and how to use them efficaciously, in aggregate, in short succession to make certain bites, are other key additives, as is importance of making ready, offering properly, accurate casting, hooking (sharpening the hooks and turning them up slightly for example to make certain that the fish stay in your hook as you reel them in), in addition to retrieving and touchdown of the fish.

An fantastic supply for novices on all matters tackle-related, system, fish species, gear and strategies, is to be observed in The Dorling Kindersley Encyclopedia of Fishing: The entire manual to the fish, tackle and techniques of clean and saltwater angling.

Our reason and cause here isn't always to restate the indexed statistics located right here. Avid and critical anglers are readers and thirst expertise in an effort to increase their odds of success. This source we suggest for young and old! (There are also a few other references indexed at the quit of this article, in case you select to pursue extra facts and or crave deeper insights into the artwork and science of Bass fishing).

All we can say, is that having highly-priced or the proper device, isn't a assure that you'll land the following huge one!In fishing, there are no real ensures. This is a 'agreement' and activity between you and nature. Exploring and getting you to the point in which you realize the feel, characteristic and embedded strengths and weaknesses of your device, is the real manner to expertise. For maximum path and blunders, exercise and persistence are the roads to comply with to turning into properly-versed and skilled anglers.

Realizing the equipments complete ability, will take time and exercise. Bear in thoughts, that sophistication in equipment will expand in parallel to your very own mastery and skill-refinement.

Your meant style of fishing (from boat or shore, shallow or deep (or each) will dictate the maximum suitable preference for tackle (reel and rod, line – thickness and weight),line, hooks, baits and lures, weights, sinkers, leaders and greater.

Whether you are a salt-water fanatic that enjoys shore, beach, boat or massive-recreation fishing or a freshwater guru, who prefer lure, bait, pole and or fly fishing, there are rod, reels, line, hooks, leaders, hyperlinks,bait, and landing address simply right for you.

Basic angling techniques are relatively easy to grasp, yet conquering and refining all the subtleties and tricky actions and maneuvers, exploring the secrets (observed or yet to be unearthed), of in this example bass fishing (which has so many iterations and settings), will take a lifetime of delight and defeat!

Practice and enjoy bass fishing, in step with your very own niche and fashion, preference and place of choice – in a phrase -YOUR 'distinctiveness'. It is a totally personalized and individualized pursuit and ardour.

Always recollect, that there is a big range of variety and entertainment on provide, by using specific sorts of fishing, locations, baits and lures and so forth., to maintain angling interesting and a developing recreation – it is contagious and pervasive – once let in, it's far hard to permit cross! You are hooked and being reeled in by means of this game and interest before you understand it.

For most anglers, technique (and preference of system) is dictated with the aid of the species sought, mounted exercise, situations and greater. Mostly artificial lures are recommended and widely wide-spread for freshwater predatory fishing. Some opt for live bait, others have fulfillment with tough baits like artificial rats and plastic worms are every other favourite.

Whether you are fishing from the banks, boat or drift tube,most might endorse you operate a six to six and a half foot (1.Eight -2m) medium, heavy-push-button, spinning or bait-casting rod and reel combination, with sturdy line (10-pound).

If you're fishing in weeds,heavy cowl, thick, slop,grassy wetlands, swamps, and many others. A heavier line (braided), will serve you better/pleasant. Hook sizes normally recommended round a # four stay-bait hook, sharpened and grew to become up slightly (say around 10%), this is completed to make certain that the fish stayed "hooked" and gives you a 'preventing' danger to reel it in and land it efficaciously.

A weed-less, # 5 hook also can serve you nicely in these conditions. Large-mouth bass can be stuck at any depth, using live baits, throughout most the yr (even ice fishing)! Sharp hooks are key.

Weights and sinkers are any other detail you ought to bear in mind, specifically in dark, cloudy waters and or while fishing deep water specially.

There also are forte sinkers, with rattles these days to lure the fish even extra. They are very sensitive to sounds, noise and vibrations within the water – so some thing you can do to create that allure, tease and temptation is great to undergo in thoughts. Do the whole thing you may to trigger their feeding response and make certain a strike/chew!

Also, consider, fish are a lot like us – on warm, humid days, they look for safe haven, meals and luxury. These are their handout and feeding floor (no extraordinary than us, trying to take a seat under an umbrella, or in the front on the TV, in an air-conditioned environment, seeking to stay cool and revel in our snack-foods!).

Knowing and thinking about those conduct, will assist you seize more fish. Look for the lily pads, think cover, giving them coloration from the sun. Find the right depth, structure and disguise-away(they generally search for cowl, like every other predator) and their lighting fixtures-rapid pace enabled them to cover water/ground speedy and without a doubt strike/attack/hit their "prey".

Weedy,shallow bays, hard-backside residences, rocks, trees and or different structures, creeks, channels, deeper waters, drops, bluffs and extra can all be part of their transferring styles and habitat, wherein they search for food. They additionally like being close to get admission to point to deeper water. More afterward their preferred spots and how to optimize these styles.

Examples of luring techniques and how the right system allow you to:

Surface, Top-water and or Buzz baits: Acting almost like a spinner bait, but with a flat blade that permits it to surface with pace, this is a famous choice for many a bass enthusiast.. It attracts the attention of the bass, with the aid of creating a disturbance along the floor like a minnow,triggering their basic feeding instincts and hunter impulse to strike. Rewarding you with a handsome trap!

Carolina Rig: this can effortlessly be defined as truly a version of the usual, so-called'Texas Rig' (see beneath),exquisite for use with plastic worms or different soft bait. Most professional bass anglers recommend using a heavier weight like 1/2 -1oz or greater.

Slide the load onto the line, observe with three plastic beads, a barrel swivel, and a frontrunner line (particularly smaller than the main line).What this permits the bass angler to do is to get the bait to 'drop down' to the floor with velocity and is particularly advocated for fishing deep waters.

The motion of the leader permits the bait to swim and rise above the bottom, and fall slowly down. For maximum novices this is easy to do and exercise and may be very flexible to get your routine rigging and address capabilities to enhance.

Crank bait: generally refers to lures, that's commonly crafted from a variety of materials, consisting of tough plastic or timber. With an introduced feature of a diving lip at the front (simulating successfully the actions of natural prey, wobbling, diving and swimming moves), entices the bass to strike. The rule of thumb, generally is that the bigger the lip, the deeper it is able to dive. Enhancements like rattles also are exact for sure situations.

Jerk baits: A pro preferred among bass anglers, for top-water, as well as suspended bass fishing. Longer minnow-shaped plugs, to be had in lots of various sizes and colors. As a floor, top-water bait with a moderate twitch-and-prevent form of retrieve, or whilst agreater sluggish-and-constant retrieves underwater. Another option is to apply postponing jerk baits that normally dive deeper, jerking it, almost teasing and tempting the bass to come up and chew proper at it.

Jigs: Some have defined those relied on address as 'lead head andhook with dressing'. Their 'brought' capabilities ought to take the shape of rubber or plastic skirts, smooth plastic baits for our bodies, as opposed to skirts. Most bass experts combine them with a frog, or a plastic bait as a "follower'(plastic trojan horse, crawfish).

Lipless Crank bait: generally regarding sinking-type lures, crafted from plastic, from time to time with many rattles inner for noise, , vibrations and causing disturbances underwater.

Poppers: Top water lures that bring long-range punch. Retrieve with those sorts of lures are fast, jerky or move in one spot for a length of time. Can be pretty powerful if you looking to figure out 'where the fish are'.

Soft Jerk bait: these can be used to great effect within the same way as a ordinary jerk bait, but may be dropped to the bottom pretty efficaciously as properly to tease out our deep-water predator, swimming around for food and dinner party.

Spinner baits: any other simulator of motion and prey on the move. It is very just like a jig, but with a blade that runs above the hook, and spins to mimic a bass favourite as well: fish.

Texas Rig: that is considered and named mainly for general rigging with aplastic malicious program. Use a sliding weight, normally bullet formed, and a hook sufficient for the scale trojan horse you have got chosen. Sharpen the hook and stick the factor of the hook immediately into the trojan horse head, convey it out the facet approximately 1/eight - 3/sixteen" below the entry, thread it again. Rotate the hook around so the factor is facing the trojan horse's frame. Lay it over the aspect to peer wherein it must enter with a purpose to hang straight. Position the work straight onto the hook if it is hanging. NOTE: if the computer virus is twisted, your line and motion will pay the priceand it will likely be much less powerful.

Walking- the-canine: that is an angling approach that generally calls for a while to master, but beginners ought to not turn away from attempting it, for it's far quite powerful with bass.

Casting over a enormously long distance, permit the bait to sit down for a quick time period, absorb the slack, and along with your rod tip pointed at the water, give it a jerk to the aspect, then at once move it backward and reel in any slack, then jerk again, and repeat all of the manner returned.

More or much less a darting from aspect-to-facet. You are in impact simulating the prey's elusive actions,enticing the hunter to comply with, stalk and hit! This might be your ace up your sleeve for hooking YOUR NEXT BIG ONE.

Slip-bobbers, rigged with a ¼ ounce plastic jig, live bait like minnow, night-crawler or leech at its tip and of direction, all on a sharpened hook

Jiggling, gently shaking, providing this near any rising weeds or brush, underwater logs, timber, stumps or cover, may additionally prove a success.

Remember that fish are constantly on the flow whilst feeding. The timing of day, quantity of sunlight, temperature of the water and greater all function into the angling equation.

Bobber-rigs or jigs are famous and pretty a success too. Slip-sinkers, Carolina (drop-shot rig) works well too.

Free-line fishing in shallow waters may additionally yield many a bass angler pretty the haul.

Casting a simple hook with live bait and feed the line to the bait, allowing it to 'swim' clearly will appeal to some sure interest. Other professionals might advise in case you are within the so-called watery salad, weeds or heavy slop, cover and jungles underwater, to move heavier is the important thing. 20 lb line the minimal and heavy-action, strong bait-casting rod and reel combinations with long, instantly handles to offer you with leverage to reel your BIG ONES in!

Floating jig-heads, with slip-sinker rig, with 2-3 foot chief have verified to be useful too, in particular while saved near the lowest, looking not to get snagged within the method. Weed-much less hooks permit you to retrieve stay-bait and or that hooked fish, thru very assume underbrush.

Again, expertise what bass absolutely eat, wherein and whilst, will help you with selecting and imparting the most effective, suitable and tempting bait (whether live or artificial). Drawing on the natural food regimen of the fish, can assist you in improving your baits and lures appearance, method, approaches and eventual fulfillment. Bass, as a predator may be looking for certain shapes, hues and familiar movement.

Plastic worms and crawfish are popular selections. Part of the motive bass is this sort of popular species to be fishing for, is they're notorious for hitting tough, biting stable and strong pulling or fighting – a sturdy recreation fish to make certain. They are acknowledged to position up a great fight.

Spinners or spoons are artificial baits which are in particular designed for the motive of tantalizing the fish. It is meant to initiate, make a strike impossible to resist, calling at the fish natural instinct to feed and or defend. It optimizes your possibilities of securing moves. Rotation, colour, skirts, fluttering movement(Lil' hustler spoiler is a favourite of many bass anglers) all paintings collectively to simulate motion and prey on the move.

Spoons act/circulate in a fishlike manner inside the water, trolled at the back of boats they're usually very powerful and also can be solid and retrieved.Plugs are made of diverse substances, designed specifically to go with the flow, dive under the floor or sink while reeling them returned or in. They simulate floor disturbance and lure fish with propellers or plastic skirts that pass and flutter within the water.

Artificial lures can be applied on my own or in mixture with live or herbal baits. The length and sort of lure will rely on the species, region and style of fishing you decide on, choose to pursue. (for instance trolling, spinning,fly-fishing).

For bass fishing specifically, a couple of recommendations are to bear in mind that engaging the predators from beneath, takes skill, exercise and persistence. For raveled weed-beds and sloppy pitches, you would possibly should tickle the surface a piece. When fishing in shallow waters, lures cast out speedy and retrieved slowly shaking it along, would possibly cause a response. It is all inside the tease and promise to the fish that look for signs and symptoms of motion inside the water.

Having a accessible pair of Polaroid sun shades are a MUST! Keep on transferring the bait around and play with the presentation – it's miles an art, obtained skill that receives higher over time. When casting the bait out, strive now not to spook the fish, remembering that they're sensitive to sound/noise, movement and vibrations. Plastic worms work nicely (round 10"). Being adaptable, switching baits, one-of-a-kind color and many others., the use of a robust Texas rig for example, hooking up a worm close to the bottom of the hook, sliding it onto the shank, popping it via, with a ½ ounce weight is probably all you need!

Having a second rod installation and ready to move or fishing with a buddy that can help you to reply quick (as the fish are constantly on the pass) and whilst they may be prepared to hit, you're prepared for them! Others endorse using braided line this is more potent than mono (for when fishing in weedy areas), with no stretch that can minimize entanglement and optimize your probabilities of retrieval through assume weeds and cowl.

Stiff rods that could withstand the "combat" bass can usually positioned up are any other base-requirement for bass fishing fanatics. Protecting your rods with rod wraps, to keep away from dings and scrapes also can maximize not simplest its performance, but maintain your angling funding in right circumstance! Shaking and popping along bait/lures,create a state of affairs that we could the fish suppose the "prey" is getting away.

However, the right system, bait, hooks and region isn't sufficient! Some primary angling techniques are required, putting in your rod and reel, knowing the fundamentals approximately tying knots for becoming a member of line to address, forming loopsand greater. Tying a comfortable knot is the primary element here, as every one ought to pose a 'weak point', that you do not need, if you have the BIG ONE hooked! Some advocate earlier than tightening a knot, to moist it with some water and trim all edges and loose ends, to avoid snag/drag.

Gulp-sinking minnows forged out rapid and far, permitting to permit it fall and dangle, quiver down,with plenty of slack,might prove just what the fish ordered! Tube-jigs, gulp-tubes that are scented, are different alternatives. The gentle,herbal-chewy substance, tricks the fish, into now not looking to allow go and feature another chew, for this reason growing your odds of landing it competently.

Top-water baits with rattles are another all-time preferred, with slack within the line, taking walks-the-dog (flipping) makes for an enticing presentation for the fish. Having a spinner-bait with some red in it, simulates blood or wounded prey to our underwater predator, triggering yet again their herbal instincts and feeding reaction, increasing your odds of getting a bite, hit or strike.

Whether you locate yourself in a jet-boat or flat-bottom bass boat, shore, rocks, seaside, cliff, flow, river, move, lake, reservoir, or different body of water, sturdy rods, warm palms, right tackle, suitable guidance, the proper bait and presentation, correct casting, in which you realize the fish is probably/pass/feed evidently, fishing for shape and sample, maintaining an eye fixed on surroundings and situations, can all make those fleeting moments of anticipation and elation at the beginning strike momentous! The fights, flights, flips, turns and jumps, attacks and difficult hits, struggles, retrieval and touchdown of bass, is what keeps us coming again!

Let us now flip to test what different concerns, plan of attack, angling strategies, secrets and techniques, mistakes and distinctiveness circumstances, can train us about the enjoyable artwork and interest, this is bass fishing!

Water, Weather, Timing And Other Environmental Aspect, Facets And Considerations For Bass Fishing

As stated all through this text thus far, there are numerous elements that we regularly do not take into account, and or brush aside, whilst we first start out, angling for bass. These would include, consideration of:

☐Water stratification and depths (bass are observed at varying degrees and knowing where (at which stage), to fish for them is paramount);shallow or deep, now and again each As some distance as water temperatures goes, at some point of a every year/seasonal cycle, waters flow, turn and gets re-oxygenized.

As temperatures fall, from deep below and for the duration of ice forms, floats to the surface, melts and moves down once more. Science has supplied us with sufficient proof that THREE wonderful layers from in a body of water – say a lake as an instance.

Deeper/less warm, Middle-ground/milder – transitional layer and the pinnacle/floor/warmer waters. Heeding those degrees and ranging temperatures, and looking oxygen-rich spots are all elements to don't forget even before heading out. Think the process through. Think like the fish might – ask your self, where would you cross possibly, in case you had been faced with the identical state of affairs – the solution will normally lead you to in which the fish most likely ARE!

A temperature gauge and intensity meter can all prepare you better, as an angler, knowledgeable and prepared, to assess the environment, higher recognize it, examine from it, and use the information you gather and feature available, because of those readings and devices, to KNOW or great decide, in which the fish could be at! Depth is a first-rate indicator of what the bass are as much as and in which they may be maximum probable discovered.

This will dictate your technique, address and how you execute your angling competencies to land THE NEXT BIG ONE! If you fish at the proper level, knowledge why the fish are there, at the pass, feeding and many others,

you will increase your odds appreciably of having moves and hooking your next huge trap. It might also be a trophy!

The depth is associated with water temperature and the optimal consolation area of the bass –

continually ask yourself, what they could opt for on a day like nowadays after which move fish there. Measure with temperature, intensity sensors, GPS etc. To set up the 'pattern' and intensity of the day.

☐ Temperature- optimal and changing

Most bass species decide on a temperate climate –their metabolism is inspired, if no longer ruled pretty a good deal via the surrounding waters they find themselves in. They can also tolerate quite a wide range of temperatures, therefore we will fish pretty a great deal all through the yr.

(60-75 degrees Fahrenheit)/ It is likewise less widely recognized that ice-fishermen hook bass at around 32-39.2 degree water temperatures, in deeper waters!When it does get chillier, they get quite extra slow, as their surroundings cools down significantly and bearing this in thoughts will yield and improve your capture.

Oxygen is also very crucial to fish. The hotter it gets, the nearer they'll live to shore, and to plant-existence, which produces oxygen and or in which they may catch the occasional breeze. Reading those indicators nature gives proper, will prepare any angler better to move in which the fish are and hook your next BIG ONE. Also search for spots that aren't too stagnant and packed with decaying flowers, as this is probably an oxygen-deprived vicinity with not a huge awareness of fish – they want to 'breathe' to stay alive too!

☐Water situations: Clarity

Clear and or murky – you'll find bass in each! Their behavior and mode of assault will alternate as they plan a way to satisfactory use up their energies inside the hunt for meals, survival etc. Predators by way of layout, they choose cover and structure and deeper waters. When spawning,) or on particularly warm days,you will maximum probable, discover them more inside the shallows.

Bass always have a 'returned-door' get right of entry to to deeper waters. These statistics ought to be able to point you in the trendy area of in which the fish are pretty aptly. The male bass is also very shielding of the nest/spawn web page and will protect it, strike at any perceived danger or intruder.

Fishing is not any extra left as much as random,contemplative, reflective trail and mistakes casting. Now, nowadays, changed with more a more driven, centered, thought-thru, rationalized and analytical aggressive technique, that attempts to understand behavior, patterns, environment, situations, time of year and so forth.

At times counting on the resource of technology and gadgets to assist and better your changes of spotting,finding, hooking, retrieving and touchdown the fish efficiently (broadly speaking in deeper waters!). Therefore, it the waters are clear, head for deeper waters as a general rule of thumb.

☐ Noise/Disturbances/Vibrations

DO NOT DISTURB symptoms are difficult to post within the water! Always keep in mind that there may be a few truth to now not chasing the fish away and being truly cautious and quiet around them. The bass mainly makes use of its entire body as a sounding board. Any surface disturbance, water motion and or displacement will entice their attention – this will in fact both assist and or hurt your angling hopes and dream.

Rusty, squeaky oars, noisy automobiles or even the sound of a fast, a ways forged might also intervene and or get their attention. Being aware about any, movement, spotting fish so to speak of their environment, matters (water, plant life) transferring around, can be accurate signs. Wearing an excellent pair of Polaroid sunglasses may help you 'see' better within the vivid sunlight and glare, reflections off the surface of the water(s).

□ Color, Sunlight, Time of day

Most bass anglers propose dawn and duck to be the pleasant feeding time for the bass – now not the height of day or whilst the solar is at it brightest and the water maybe a diploma ortoo warm for our fishy pals and when they head for the deep and or cover. It is a matter of attractive to their natural instincts.

They are eager observers and movement and shade were researched within the bass species. Picking presentation of bait, lure that is closest to live or alive bait, resembles their prey, in different phrases, will maximize your possibilities of catching extra bass. This does now not imply that they may no longer strike at night as an example or at different times at some stage in the day – you might just must adapt and use a few specialist strategies to lure them out of hiding a bit!

☐ Time of 12 months: Seasons and things are a changing!

Surroundings, weather and angling guidelines trade and preserve converting. The stage and gamers do not continue to be the same and even on the equal day,each day, things will range. This variety (the spice of lifestyles most say) is what keeps most of us guessing, adapting, changing approach,bait, intensity and so on. All within the endured hope and pursuit of catching the NEXT BIG ONE.

As to the first-class time to seize bass – reviews range greatly in this subject matter. In a few areas, fishing is handiest allowed after spawning.

Spring, summer time and fall (with fall being the satisfactory for most larger fish) and even iciness a few shape of bass fishing is available to you, depending on where you are, what the climate situations are like and what sort of 12 months the bass are having (spawning fulfillment, fitness of the frame of water they live and thrive in, the eco-system, stocking, pollutants and so on.) Even ice fishing is feasible (greater about this beneath forte fishing in the direction of the quit of the text).

As mentioned earlier, climate influences conduct and the season and type of water, would possibly all require extraordinary technique, system and bait and lures/coaching AND presentation.

As an angler, avid bass angler, this could not faze you in any manner! On the opposite, it presents you with the opportunity to shift gears, alternate strategy, tools, refine competencies, research extra approximately your opponent and its conduct.

By being alert, conscious and observant, you'll learn a lot about the fish – it is no longer a passive sport! Windy, low and or excessive air pressure, water temperature, uneven waves and or floor motion of the water,cloudy skies, with lots of cloud cover, covering the solar, should dictate whether or not fish can be biting or not, color of plastic worms might be adjusted from blue (on bright days), to black (on cloudy days with now not numerous sun round). Modifying your fishing techniques and adapting to climate patterns, even adjusting your bait/lures, strategy,all undergo witness of an alert bass master!

Bass also are touchy to very vibrant sunlight, so then you definitely would possibly discover them searching out a few shady cover and or cooler waters. That expertise will put together you properly for where to head and look for them. Increasing your odds of finding them too!

☐Predatory Nature and creatures of dependancy – what the fish themselves inform us (or not!)

There predators of the deep are wealthy of their existence cycles, conduct and patters. It is their nature after-all. They are extremely predictable. As hunters, they do positive matters, instinctively and as anglers, we capitalize on it.

There are plenty of records approximately the species, really worth knowing and key to know-how – the secret to unlocking the fulfillment of bass fishing. Thinking like a hunter ourselves and at times like the fish, can increase your odds and success considerably. Being one with nature and its problematic styles, conduct, balance and quirkiness, allow fisherman to be professional, unique, properly organized and extra successful, in place of leaving it as much as eventuality and random risk to relaxed a chew!

☐ Preferred habitat and fishing systems

One author likens contour and topographic maps to bass fishermen, like treasure maps to pirates once had been. Lines display elevation, intensity etc. Get an idea of what the 'ground' or backside of the frame of water (like a lake for instance) could look like – it's far not often flat, frequently characterized with the aid of rises and humps, slopes and drop-offs.

Slopes and access-factors into deeper water have to also yield more frequent, larger hauls and more strikes, as bass opt to have get right of entry to to deeper waters and are continuously at the pass, looking and feeding and or protecting territory.

☐Natural Diet and Menu– the artwork of attractive fish: developing the proper environment/situations/charm for a strike

Lots have already been said about this subject matter.

☐Self Self assurance

The notion for your ability to find and catch the diverse bass species, is by using far the satisfactory device of the exchange to foster and broaden over time. This can't be purchased and is the private call to every fisherman, to include in his/her address-box!

Whether you pick out to use spinners, or swear by plastic worms, crawfish and other live bait, chum or have a favourite trap for motives and or secrets which might be your very very own, you use what works the pleasant and what you accept as true with will produce the bass you need, preference and need to have!

Positive mindset is going an extended way whilst getting to know how to fish for bass. Profiting from on-going enjoy, fulfillment and failure, your angling and odds will maintain improving. Practice in this case, will move a protracted way to permit success in this unpredictable,various situation – while you are one-on-one with the maximum popular recreation and wearing fish of all of them: The Bass itself!

Techniques For Bass Fishing Like A Pro (Worms,Skipping, Ripping, Drift Trolling, Flyrodding)

The artwork of correct casting

Mastering primary casting is key. Most spinning and bait-casting reel and rod combos nowadays, are made for hassle-free, ease-of-use flexibility via a variety of anglers (multi-level at that too!)

Try to eliminate mistakes from your basic fashion and method. Skill and accuracy must matter extra than strength and it isn't continually about getting it as a ways out, as fast as you in all likelihood can (despite the fact that this might be crucial in sure conditions and situations too!)

Casting, getting your line/hook/bait,sinkers, weights and leaders in and into the water, at the precise proper intensity, imitating 'prey', and doing so with severe, pin-factor accuracy, is what that is all approximately. Hitting your target with self assurance is a very simple talent to grasp and refine. Getting the hook out to precisely in which you desired it to be, what you ought to practice and work for.

Casting is one part of this manner, getting the trap to the proper depth pretty every other. Advanced bass anglers advise the usage of a countdown OR counting technique. Quite easy simply. Form the instant the bait hits the water, begin counting, one thousand, 1000 and 1, a thousand and a pair of, one thousand and three… estimating the seconds it'll take for it to 'drop' into the water.

This will help you realize higher what you are doing, when it hits the bottom as an example, whether or not it were given stuck on some thing inside the method etc. YOU set up reference factors for your self on and in the water.

Hands-on and rod in-hand is the fine way. Practice-plugs within the park, or your very own backyard (be it on 'dry land', so to speak), will make you that more powerful and correct, in and at the water, irrespective of what the body of water, or style of fishing you select to pursue. Whether spinning, bait casing or fly-rodding, there is something for each taste. Even overlooked objectives, attempts and failure,are also top instructors, as this method is incredibly of a habitual you may grasp and examine.

Casting a lure with a spinning reel as an instance, casting glide and or leger rig, bait casting are very similar. Lure fishing, spinning, floating, spoons, plugs, surface or pinnacle-water lures, crank bait, trolling etc.

Are all basic strategies that require publicity, brief demos and palms-on practice. We advocate a video or DVD, or on line in-depth rationalization, looking a fishing display or and getting hints from different anglers and professionals, as well as locating and defining your very own fashion which you are comfortable and a success with. The beauty of bass fishing, is that it gives something for all and sundry, irrespective of what your prior experience with fishing might be!

Focusing in your grip, spinning reels, bait-casters and or closed-face spin casters techniques and mastery, picking a target, aiming to land your lure (terminal tackle) in the center of that target, is a superb method.

As a widespread rule of thumb, an amazing arch inside the air as a tour path en route to the water, is a good reference and desires to have, as you set out to enhance your casting technique and accuracy.Line-manipulate is important to keep away from overshooting, get a gentler touchdown, slow flight (with the aid of touching the lip of the spool with the end of your index finger (also regarded to anglers as 'feathering') is useful.

Playing and touchdown fish

Getting to understand the texture of a fish in your hook,line and rod may be very crucial. Retrieval is about extra than sincerely getting the fish into the eager hands/internet/boat. Mastery, maneuvering, responsiveness,understanding of your address, nicely-balanced manipulate,reel-clutching, preventing curves and arching/bending rods and the various controls and settings, strategies (which include casting, hooking, gambling, reeling in, retrieving and landing is vital.

They are so much more than mere steps in a technique and or sum-general of elements. To translate into a true blue-blood bass-fishing revel in and success, appreciation of the symphony of the interplay of process and final results, tactic, technique, angler, gadget, the capture and haul is what's at play right here.

When the usage of a spinning reel/bait-casting, there are three key strategies to grasp that would consist of reel control:

with anti-reverse on, returned winding (anti-opposite off) and thumb-strain control

There is not anything more thrilling than a fish at the run, observe strain, hold the rod up barely and growth the 'drag' if required, the use of one of the techniques above. Watch tension and keep away from line-breaks and permit the fish to tire.

It is one aspect to put together,cast, tease and tempt, hook and in the end reel in. The process however does no longer forestall there. More of the simple technique mastery includes strategies of touchdown fish, like beaching (no longer appropriate for trap and launch), tailing (now not proper for all species), lipping (watch the teethed species here!), netting or even gaffing (banned in maximum regions, due to the risk of the stroke injuring the fish).

The maximum beneficial tip we will provide or endorse, is ultimate on top of things, alert and now not disillusioned or startle the fish even more. Allow the worn-out fish to show, submerge the internet and avoid lunging at it.

When lipping, grip the decrease lip gently among your thumb and forefingers, unhook carefully or keep in the water while freeing it lightly, but successfully, with out hurting the fish, adhering as a ways as viable,to present day and well-known, capture-and-launch practices.

Lure-fishing and spinning

Spinning address and artificial baits and lures are growing in reputation and the most popular shape of fishing global. As far as bass fishing is concerned, one of the simplest way to attract the species – even for beginners and novice anglers of all ages and fishing fashion and ability-tiers.

Rotation, shade and movement, staying as actual as you can to the natural diet and target prey of the bass will optimize your chances.The form and thickness of the spinning 'blade' at the lure influences the motion and mobility of the trap – how it responds and acts in and beneath water.

Floating lures are also not unusual and effective particularly for deep-water bass fishing. Watch for snagging on the bottom and make sure to weigh it executed as it should be the usage of appropriate weights. This method guarantees getting the bait at eye-degree of the fish.

For spoons, there arewide categories, specifically trolling and casting spoons. Weed-much lesslures in most cases have hooks with nylon or steel weed-guards that save you snagging and or non-weedless spoons also are typically used. How to inform which one to use, most bass anglers look for shape, weight and pace.

The first-rate way to locate your way around in any tackle save or field, is to practice and get to realize the conduct and or success in one-of-a-kind situations. Trying to get to know the highest quality retrieval and fulfillment costs, perhaps even logging it in a personal journal as you adopt your bass adventure/hunt for the NEXT BIG ONE!

Plugs, floor lures,useful at all fishing stages, in any respect speeds make those lures versatile, agile and an all-time favored of many a bass angler.

Matching the lure to the conditions you face and the situation, body of water and particular species you're fishing for (small-mouth,big-mouth, striped, noticed, rock, yellow, black, white and so on.). Shallow-diving crank-bait and or floor or pinnacle-water lures have tested themselves only for bass fishing – fantastic for fishing shallows.

Stick-baits and jerking, minnow plugs (or the real thing!), prop-baits, surface disturbers, crawler-type top-water baits and even a floating, riding crank-bait can prove useful.

The true secret lies in what a few call the 'one-punch' – teasing and engaging with a top-water or teaser (surface disturber) after which following it up with a plastic computer virus as an example on a 2nd rod, for optimizing strikes and yet again tipping the scales for your choose.

Plastic worms

There are a massive array of worms to be had in the marketplace (both live bait and artificial). For avid bass anglers they are a need. The method to master is hooking them properly. When hooking a trojan horse for bass fishing, it's far of extreme importance to make sure which you thread it properly.

Get a variety of the frame onto the hook, hooking it twice, at top and backside. This is to make sure that it does now not fly unfastened while you are casting it out into the water. It also protects it quite within the submerged paradise that the bass stocks with different fish, who may want to come back and take a chew or sample!

www.ingramcontent.com/pod-product-compliance
Lightning Source LLC
Chambersburg PA
CBHW060326030426
42336CB00011B/1221